ORTHO'S All About

Garden Pools
and Fountains

Written by Veronica Lorson Fowler and Jamie Beyer

Meredith® Books
Des Moines, Iowa

Ortho® Books
An imprint of Meredith® Books

All About Garden Pools and Fountains
Editor: Marilyn Rogers
Contributing Editor: Leona H. Openshaw
Contributing Technical Editors: Jamie Beyer,
   William C. Uber
Art Director: Tom Wegner
Copy Chief: Catherine Hamrick
Copy and Production Editor: Terri Fredrickson
Contributing Copy Editors: Martin Miller, Carol Boker
Contributing Proofreaders: Kathy Roth Eastman,
   Steve Hallam, Margaret Smith,
Contributing Map Illustrator: Jana Fothergill
Contributing Prop/Photo Stylist: Mary E. Klingaman
Indexer: Don Glassman
Electronic Production Coordinator: Paula Forest
Editorial and Design Assistants: Kathleen Stevens,
   Karen Schirm
Production Director: Douglas M. Johnston
Production Manager: Pam Kvitne
Assistant Prepress Manager: Marjorie J. Schenkelberg

Additional Editorial Contributions from
   Art Rep Services
Director: Chip Nadeau
Designers: lk Design, Shawn Wallace
Illustrators: Rick Hanson

Meredith® Books
Editor in Chief: James D. Blume
Design Director: Matt Strelecki
Managing Editor: Gregory H. Kayko
Executive Ortho Editor: Benjamin W. Allen

Director, Sales & Marketing, Retail: Michael A. Peterson
Director, Sales & Marketing, Special Markets:
   Rita McMullen
Director, Sales & Marketing, Home & Garden Center
   Channel: Ray Wolf
Director, Operations: George A. Susral

Vice President, General Manager: Jamie L. Martin

Meredith Publishing Group
President, Publishing Group: Christopher M. Little
Vice President, Consumer Marketing & Development:
   Hal Oringer

Meredith Corporation
Chairman and Chief Executive Officer: William T. Kerr
Chairman of the Executive Committee: E.T. Meredith III

Cover photograph: Jerry Howard/Positive Images

All of us at Ortho® Books are dedicated to providing you
with the information and ideas you need to enhance your
home and garden. We welcome your comments and
suggestions about this book. Write to us at:
   Meredith Corporation
   Ortho Books
   1716 Locust St.
   Des Moines, IA 50309–3023

If you would like more information on other Ortho
products, call 800-225-2883 or visit us at www.ortho.com

Thanks to
Janet Anderson, Laura Davenport, Melissa George, Lori
Gould, Ann Hiemstra, Colleen Johnson, Aimee Reiman,
Mary Irene Swartz; Water Creations, Des Moines, Iowa

Photographers
(Photographers credited may retain copyright ©
   to the listed photographs.)
L= Left, R= Right, C= Center, B= Bottom, T= Top
Cathy Wilkinson Barash: p. 68, 79 (R2);
David Cavagnaro: p. 13 (R3), 78 (L5), 79 (R3, R4);
R. Todd Davis: p. 12, 13 (R1);
E. R. Degginger/Color-Pic, Inc.: p. 77 (R2);
Alan & Linda Detrick: p. 33 (BL);
Catriona Tudor Erler: p. 57, 60;
Derek Fell: p. 80 (L4), 87T;
T.L. Gettings: p. 77 (R5), 80 (L1, L2, L3, & L5), 84 (T);
John Glover: p. 8, 9 (T, BL), 10 (L, (BR), 13 (R5), 14, 32,
   33 (TL, BR), 37 (BR), 39 (TL, TR), 54, 56 (L), 61 (B),
   79 (R1);
David Goldberg: p. 34, 35, 45;
Jerry Harpur: p. 11 (CL), 39 (B), 51;
Lynne Harrison: p. 11 (TR);
C. B. Hellquist: p. 77 (R3, R4);
Jerry Howard/Positive Images: p. 9 (BR), 36 (T);
judywhite/New Leaf Images: p. 76 (L1, L2);
Dency Kane: p. 74;
Lynn Karlin: p. 43;
Andrew Lawson: p. 52, 53 (L), 77 (R1), 78 (L4), 79 (R5,
   R6), 84 (B);
Lilypons Water Gardens: p. 76 (L4), 77 (R6);
Julie Maris/Semel: p. 11 (CR, BL), 37 (BL);
Marilynn Mc Ara: p. 38 (T), 61 (T);
Bryan McCay: p. 3 (C), 16-17, 19, 20, 30, 46, 65, 75, 86;
David McDonald/PhotoGarden: p. 15, 72–73, 89;
Clive Nichols: p. 40 (Brook Cottage, Oxfordshire),
   56R (Anthony Noel), 59 (Jill Billington);
Susan A. Roth: p. 33 (TR), 53 (R), 81;
Richard Shiell: p. 78 (L2);
Albert Squillace/Positive Images: p. 13 (R2);
The Studio Central: p. 23, 24, 25, 26, 28, 29, 64, 69;
Michael S. Thompson: p. 3 (B), 6, 10 (CR), 13 (R4),
   76 (L3), 78 (L1), 82 (L);
Van Ness Water Gardens: p. 13 (L), 77.

Note to the Readers: Due to differing conditions, tools,
and individual skills, Meredith Corporation assumes no
responsibility for any damages, injuries suffered, or losses
incurred as a result of following the information published
in this book. Before beginning any project, review the
instructions carefully, and if any doubts or questions remain,
consult local experts or authorities. Because codes and
regulations vary greatly, you always should check with
authorities to ensure that your project complies with all
applicable local codes and regulations. Always read and
observe all of the safety precautions provided by
manufacturers of any tools, equipment, or supplies,
and follow all accepted safety procedures.

PLANNING YOUR GARDEN POOL

The sparkle of a stream, the splashing of a fountain, the glimpse of golden fish, the delicate petals of a water lily—all these and more are reasons to add water to your landscape.

A water feature can be as simple as a wooden tub or as elaborate as a stream with bridges, waterfalls and pools of exotic plants and fish. It can be a formal tiered fountain centered in a patio, or a pool so natural your guests will assume it's always been there. And most water features—no matter what type you choose—are terrific do-it-yourself projects.

Water gardens were favorites of the Moors, for whom water was a symbol of life and purity. They positioned cooling fountains in the middle of their formal courtyards to signify the primacy of water. Early Asians, too, valued water gardens as an aid to meditation and delighted in breeding rare fish. In ancient times, Chinese nobility would spend their afternoons lolling in small boats on water gardens while servants floated tea-filled cups to them on lily pads. For Renaissance Italians, water was a toy. They loved ornate fountains and whimsical sprays—some designed to squirt unsuspecting strollers—and installed them throughout their estates.

Today, water gardens have again grown popular, even in our humbler yards. Like the gardeners before them, modern homeowners find that water features are beautiful and peaceful additions to the landscape. Unlike the past, today's gardeners have better tools and materials with which to build their pools. Flexible and preformed liner materials, for example, have revolutionized design and scaled down installation.

Water gardening is easier than ever, and even if you're an amateur, building a garden pond today is limited less by your wallet than it is by your imagination.

Once, you might have only dreamt you could have a water garden this beautiful. Now you can build it yourself. It takes planning and effort, but the end result will transform your backyard landscape.

FEASIBILITY FIRST

When tackling a large project, such as this one, be prepared for the cost, time, and expertise it will require over the years.

A water garden will go anywhere—in the yard, on the patio, on a balcony, or a porch—even indoors. But certain water features are better suited than others to certain sites (and to certain gardeners, for that matter).

WHAT IS FEASIBLE?

This should be your first question, and to find out which water feature best suits you, your resources, and your space, you'll need to educate yourself. Be a "know it all" before you start, and you will be well prepared to begin your water garden.

Read this book from cover to cover; there's a wealth of information on everything from principles of design to pumps and plants. Browse through water garden catalogs, too; check out prices and calculate what you can afford. Call water garden suppliers and ask questions about their products. If possible, visit local water gardens. Talk with the owners or those who care for them. Visit local clubs—many communities have organizations that sponsor tours.

If you're well informed, you'll make better plans, find installation easier, and prevent frustrations down the road.

SIZE AND SITE

First, check out your site. A large water garden with a spectacular waterfall will overwhelm a small lot. It also might overwork your budget, your time, and your back. A small garden pool, on the other hand, could get lost in an expansive landscape.

If you're planning anything more involved than a premade fountain or container water garden, you'll also need to check with city or county offices to find out if there are any ordinances that apply to the installation of water gardens. Depending on the depth, you may need to fence it (some cities require a

THE COSTS

Note: Prices are approximate and will vary depending on the quality of materials and the region.

- Mid-quality flexible liner: $1 per square foot
- Mid-quality pump for a small pool: $75–$150
- Flagstone: $2.50 per square foot
- Fountain head: $25
- 8-foot by 4-foot kidney-shaped preformed plastic liner: $400
- Plants for a 3-foot by 5-foot garden: $150
- Biofilter: $100–$3,500
- Premade 6-foot wooden bridge: $700
- Professionally installed GFI electrical source: $100
- A tub garden with small fountain: $200
- A 3-foot by 5-foot in-ground garden with flexible liner, a small fountain, and stone edging: $500
- A formal three-tiered fountain: $800
- A self-installed 10-foot by 20-foot in-ground garden with flexible liner, and a medium-sized fountain: $2,000
- A self-installed 20-foot by 30-foot in-ground garden with 20-foot stone-landscaped stream and waterfalls: $3,500

HINT

If you want your first water garden to be a large one, consider consulting a landscape architect or water-garden specialist to help you design it and to estimate how much of its installation you can accomplish by yourself. You'll save money in the long run by avoiding costly mistakes.

6-foot fence for anything deeper than 18 inches). You may need to install it at a specified distance from property lines, especially if it's above ground. Check to see if there are limitations on size, height, and lighting for water features. Remember that both plumbing and electrical work will need to meet local codes.

BE CALCULATING

Figure all costs in advance. Small gardens are inexpensive, but large gardens can cost thousands of dollars. You don't want to find yourself in the position of the would-be water gardener who dug a large hole one spring weekend only to fill it in again because the liner was too expensive and didn't fit in the budget.

You may need to contract a large project (or parts of it) to a professional. Pouring concrete, installing electric lines, bricklaying, and excavation can be extensive (and expensive) and are jobs best left to the pros.

Assess your time and strength. A tub garden will take an hour or two to put together, but a large water garden may take weeks to dig and build. It will also require a good back and strong arms and legs. An 18-inch-deep, 6-foot by 4-foot hole may not sound like a big job, but it would probably take a middle-aged man of average strength a half day to dig. Soil disposal could take another half day, depending on what you do with it. Ask relatives or friends to help dig, or hire a neighborhood teen for the job. For large projects, you can rent a backhoe.

Remember to calculate maintenance time, too. A tub garden with a water lily takes just a few minutes a week. So does a freestanding or a wall fountain. Add plants and fish and you add more time. A garden just a few feet across with a few plants and fish will need your attention for an hour or less each week. Larger gardens can demand two or three hours a week or more.

SAFETY TIPS

- **Err on the side of caution.** If you're unsure about your ability to perform a procedure safely, hire a professional.
- **Wear safety goggles** when working on anything that sends debris flying—especially when cutting wood or stone.
- **Wear protective clothing**—such as leather gloves—when moving stone. Wear sturdy steel-toed shoes or boots when digging, cutting, or carrying heavy objects. When working in the sun, wear a hat and a lightweight shirt, and be sure to apply sunblock.
- **Don't work at night,** even with outdoor lighting. It's too easy to make a mistake when it is difficult to see what you're doing.
- **Invest in the right tools.** They'll make the job easier and the result will be more professional looking. Also, by using the proper tool for the job, you'll avoid injuries.
- **Keep kids away.** Power tools, water, electricity, and children don't mix.
- **Stay cool.** When working in the heat, take frequent breaks and drink plenty of liquids.

The proper building techniques make the difference between a well-functioning water garden and one with chronic problems.

SHOULD YOU HIRE IT OUT? A SKILLS RANKING.

EASY ENOUGH FOR BEGINNERS
- Sealing and installing a pump in a container
- Digging a hole a few feet across
- Laying flagstone or stacking concrete paving blocks
- Installing narrow widths of flexible or preformed liner
- Creating a bog garden
- Working with sand, gravel, and boulders less than 1 foot in diameter

INTERMEDIATE SKILLS
- Installing a freestanding fountain
- Building a stream or waterfall
- Laying a brick patio
- Laying small amounts of tile

- Working with medium-sized boulders and rocks 1 to 3 feet in diameter
- Building a wood-sided water garden

CHALLENGING
- Installing a wall fountain
- Installing a bridge
- Working with large boulders and rocks more than 3 feet in diameter

FOR PROFESSIONALS (OR HIGHLY SKILLED AMATEURS)
- Wiring and other electrical work
- Operating a backhoe
- Laying brick and concrete block
- Installing 1-foot or higher stone walls
- Pouring concrete

WHICH STYLE FOR YOU?

Beautifully situated in the landscape, this pool is obviously the result of planning.

Water features are as individual as the gardeners who create them. Ask yourself the following questions to help you decide which is best for you.

WHAT SIZE?

■ Do I have an hour or two (or more) each week to devote to water gardening?
■ Is my landscape fairly large?
■ Have I installed a water garden before?
■ Am I a fairly experienced do-it-yourselfer?
■ Do I have friends or family who can help?
■ Will my budget let me spend several hundred dollars or more on a water feature?

If you answered "no" to most of the questions, you should build a small pond.

HINT

What kind of water feature will please you the most? To answer that question, visit the library or bookstore and stock up on water garden books. Note the dozen or so water features you like best. Review these favorites and look for similarities. Those are the characteristics you'll want to work into your water garden.

FORMAL OR INFORMAL?

■ Do I like straight lines and symmetry?
■ Does my landscape already have a number of formal elements?
■ Do I thrive on order?
■ Is my lot a geometric shape?

■ Do the doors and windows of my house look out on a landscape designed in grids?
■ Is my home interior formal?
■ Do I find some informal gardens disorderly?

If you answered "yes" to most questions, you lean toward a formal garden pool.

ABOVE GROUND OR IN GROUND?

■ Will digging the garden be difficult?
■ Would I like the water garden located near a sitting area, and should the water be at eye-level when I'm seated?
■ Is the water table high in my area?
■ Do I live in a reasonably mild climate?
■ Is the site in a low spot that might flood if the water feature isn't above ground?

The more "yes" answers, the more an aboveground pool is appropriate for your site; the more "no" answers, the more an in-ground pool is the better choice.

WHICH FEATURES?

■ Do I want the sound of splashing water?
■ Will I keep fish in the water garden?
■ Do I want to see moving water or watch it course through my landscape?
■ Is the site calm, not buffeted by winds that might disturb a fountain or high waterfall?

If you answered "yes" to most questions, include a fountain, stream, or waterfall in your plans.

DO I WANT PLANTS?

■ Will the garden receive four or more hours of sunlight?
■ Am I interested in tending new plants?
■ Do I want fish?
■ Am I concerned about keeping the water clear without chemicals?
■ Am I willing to spend extra time on plants?

If you answered "yes" to most questions, add plants to your pond.

SHOULD I HAVE FISH IN MY GARDEN?

■ Do I live in a mild climate; if not, am I willing to overwinter the fish?
■ Am I willing to provide the extra weekly care that fish require?
■ Do I want to minimize mosquitoes?
■ Is having a complete, self-regulating ecosystem important to me?

If you answered "yes" to most questions, add fish to your pond.

FORMAL AND INFORMAL

Garden styles can be categorized as formal or informal, and water gardens are no exception.

Formal gardens are symmetrical and fit into landscapes designed in grids. They tend to be straight-lined and angular and lend themselves especially well to traditional homes and formal urban landscapes. Their well-ordered appearance is enhanced with rectangular or square materials—brick, cut stone, marble, and ceramic tile. Most wall fountains and freestanding fountains are formal, although as water features become increasingly popular, more informal fountains are available.

Informal gardens are the opposite of formal gardens. They often have an abstract shape and are set casually or asymmetrically into country gardens and medium-sized yards. Because of their naturalistic look, it's critical that they blend into the surrounding landscape as a part of beds, borders, decks, or at the edge of woodlands. Informal water garden materials tend to be round or irregular—flagstone, wood, boulders, rock, and gravel.

A formal pool fits neatly into a small, rectangular patio.

This informal water feature, full of curves and turns, is a natural for a wooded lot and a casual, nature-oriented lifestyle.

IN GROUND VERSUS ABOVE GROUND

In-ground pools are good projects for beginning water gardeners because their installation generally doesn't require special skills. Aside from digging and hauling soil away, building one is simple—dig it, line it, and fill it. Even when small, they are attractive and fit into both naturalistic and formal landscapes.

Aboveground pools have advantages, too; however, their installation is not without effort. They're excellent for areas where you want the water close to eye level or situated at just the right height for dangling fingers.

Aboveground pools are ideal for those difficult-to-dig locations in clay, compacted soil, or among tree roots. They are suited to mild climates where water doesn't freeze and where footings can be set less thick and deep.

Although some aboveground pools require little digging (others, none at all), you still have to build its sides and, depending on the style you choose, this can take skill. The sides can be built from almost any material: brick, stone, concrete, tile, wood, even flower-border edging purchased at a garden center.

WHICH STYLE FOR YOU?
continued

A GALLERY OF STYLE

No matter how small or how large, all water features add a special element to a landscape. But how do you go about adding that splash, sparkle, and movement to your landscape? Think creatively. Take a cue from the water features on this page; they incorporate interesting objects—sculpture, urns, and furniture—and fit the overall feeling of the landscape in which they appear. Consider converting water-tight containers into self-contained fountains, or come up with your own original shape or design. After all, a water garden reflects more than the sky above—it also reflects your personality.

Decks can be the perfect spot for garden pools. You can incorporate pools into the design of your new deck or add one to an existing area. This deck brings a formal, modernistic note to an otherwise informal landscape.

Existing materials often dictate design. This brick-edged pool is an orderly, logical extension of the brick patio.

A bubbler transforms this urn into a small container fountain—ideal for gardeners with limited time, money, and space.

The formal fountain at right, surrounded by a hodge-podge of flowers and accessories, is decidedly friendly.

Water gardens don't get much smaller— or more charming—than this. A tiny, shallow pool has been tucked cleverly into a flower bed.

The pool at left not only punctuates the stone patio beautifully, it also creates a lovely view from the house.

Sometimes, the most creative garden pool accessories, such as this leafy waterfall, can be found through local crafts people.

This pond looks as though Mother Nature herself created it. It's an ideal attraction for a wide variety of wildlife and a great spot for fish.

Tucked into a corner of the garden and paired with an inviting bench, this tiny pool is small on size yet big on relaxation.

This simple stock tank has been painted and planted to become the focal point of the garden.

POOLS FOR WILDLIFE

Build it and they will come. Water is instantly a host to numerous forms of wildlife.

No matter what type of feature you install, it will attract wildlife. Birds will take a sip of water from even a simple tub, and they'll bathe in a splashing fountain. Butterflies love shallow pools. Insects and other animals—dragonflies, frogs, salamanders—will be drawn to your water feature and to the plants that accompany it.

Of course, water gardens may also attract visitors you would rather not deal with—raccoons, mosquitoes, cats that love fish, and even the occasional rambunctious, water-loving dog. But all in all, water gardens extend the ecosystem delightfully into your own backyard.

Water gardens in a country setting may attract abundant wildlife because animals are more plentiful in locations near their natural habitat. Yet even a big-city water garden draws birds, butterflies, and other animals.

A large garden may attract a more diverse selection of wild things, but a small garden will surprise you with the number of animals it lures.

Wildlife won't know whether your garden is formal or informal, of course. But the more that it resembles a country pond, the greater the number and variety of creatures it will attract because of the greater variety of habitats it offers.

Although the location, style, and size of your garden all contribute somewhat to your success with wildlife, so will having a diversity of depths, rocks, and plants.

DEPTH

If you're planning a pool that will support fish and plants as well as other wildlife activity, you'll need to consider constructing it to contain a variety of depths. Fish need at least 18 inches of water to survive. To overwinter them in areas where the pool freezes, they will need a place on the bottom deeper than that. Plants overwintering in the garden pond will need deep areas, too.

In a climate with winter temperatures of minus 10° to minus 20° F, the pond will need to be 24 inches deep. In regions where average minimum temperatures of minus 30° to minus 40° F, the pool should have areas that are 30 to 36 inches deep. Check with your local extension service or water garden supplier to be sure the garden pool you're planning will have depths suitable to your garden and your region.

Many amphibians, small animals, and birds like gradual approaches to water. An inclined beach of small stones provides a natural entry into the pool for them, and you may want to

A POOL TO ATTRACT WILDLIFE

Pebble beach
Gentle slope lets animals approach water gradually

Floating plants
Shade water and provide landing pads for insects

Rock basking places
Attract butterflies to warm themselves

Trees and shrubs
Attract beneficial insects, provide wildlife food and cover

Food for water fowl
Includes duckweed and duck potato

Grasses
Provide cover near water year-round

Rock nooks and crannies
Give amphibians cool spots in summer and hibernation spots in winter

Wildlife-attracting marginal and bog plants
Provide food and nectar for a wide variety of animals

Frogs can be purchased through water garden suppliers— or they might show up on their own.

include one in your plans (see page 41 for additional information).

ROCKS

Rocks and stones at the edge of your garden pond are welcome mats for wildlife. Butterflies and small amphibians will bask in the morning sun on low, flat stones. Large stones near the edges serve as perches for water birds. Stones with nooks and crannies, submerged or placed on edge, make shady summer havens for amphibians and protected sites for them to hibernate in winter.

PLANTS

Native plants, which offer food and shelter natural to the birds and animals of your region, draw wildlife to your garden pond. Trees and shrubs are especially good because they provide homes for nesting wildlife as well as food and cover.

   Perennials and annuals are attractions, too. Their patches of color draw birds and butterflies to feed on seeds and flower nectar. Grasses and sedges, especially evergreen or semievergreen species, provide cover at the water's edge for the better part of the year. Marginal plants (those that grow in the shallows of the pool) also offer cover and food. Plants with floating leaves shade the water and serve as insect landing pads. Those with smaller leaves, like duckweed, are food for ducks and fish. Submerged plants release small amounts of oxygen into the water, which support insect larvae.

   Bog gardens are ideal for water-loving birds and insects, providing puddles from which butterflies can sip.

HINT

In a pool where aquatic plants and fish are properly balanced, algae remain under control (providing some food and cover), the water takes on a clear greenish color, and you should be able to see your hand when you hold it about 6 inches under the water.

PLANTS FOR ATTRACTING WILDLIFE

NOTE: The following are perennial unless otherwise noted.

■ **Cardinal flower** (*Lobelia cardinalis*) grows about 3 feet high and shows off bright red flowers in late summer and early fall. A marginal or bog plant, it likes full sun. Zones 3–8.

Cardinal flower

■ **Parrot's feather and water milfoil** (*Myriophyllum* spp.) are plants that grow partially submerged along the edge of a pond and like full to partial sun. Some of the species help oxygenate the water for fish; all provide an excellent area for spawning. Zones 5–10.

Parrot's feather

■ **Swamp milkweed or butterfly plant** (*Asclepias incarnata*) grows about 3 feet high, and its yellow-to-orange, red, yellow, or white flowers attract butterflies with nectar. It's a full-sun bog plant. Zones 3–9.

Swamp milkweed

■ **Water mint** (*Mentha aquatica*) grows about 1 foot high and bears small, light lavender flowers in mid- to late summer with nectar that is attractive to bees. It spreads rapidly and can be invasive. A marginal, it should be planted no deeper than 3 inches. Zones 4–10.

Water mint

■ **Water lily** (*Nymphaea* spp.) spreads from 1 to 50 square feet, depending on the variety. Its flowers come in many colors and grow from 1 to 10 inches across. It prefers full sun and still water and makes a good place for frogs and other small animals to rest. Hardiness depends on the variety, but most hardy water lilies can be grown in zones 4–10.

Water lily

GARDEN POOLS AND CHILDREN

Just because you have children—or frequent visits from children— doesn't mean you can't have a water feature. This bubbler fountain surrounded with stones has no pooling water in which a little one can come to harm.

One of the biggest concerns about water gardening is the safety of small children. A toddler can drown in just an inch of water or in a partly filled 5-gallon bucket. No wonder that parents, grandparents, and neighbors are fearful around any kind of water feature.

No water garden can be made absolutely childproof, but there are a number of ways you can make yours safer. Shallow pools, fountains designed for safety, strategically placed boulders, and fencing help children and water gardens to coexist with less worry. Of course, you should never leave children unattended even around shallow water or the most carefully designed water feature.

No water garden is childproof, but this feature comes close. Pooled water is minimal. Reservoirs where water would normally pool are filled with attractive stones.

Keep in mind that safety is dependent somewhat on age—a garden that is safe for older children may not be safe for toddlers. You may feel confident that a 5-year-old is safe near a half-whiskey-barrel tub garden, but don't expect an 18-month-old to be.

Even 8- and 9-year-olds should be supervised near water gardens that have 3 feet or more of water. It's a mistake to believe you can create a large pond and train children to stay away from it. The same attractions that draw adults—splashing water, pretty fish, the joy of dangling a hand in cool water—entice the best-behaved children. And even well-trained children have friends or neighbors who will be drawn to your water garden.

Although you should make sure your homeowner's insurance will cover a water garden accident, the best approach is to design the pool so that tragedy doesn't happen in the first place.

FENCING

A fence—as long as it surrounds the pool and has a childproof or locked gate—allows you to have peace of mind with any kind of water garden that you want. Pretty picket fencing, 6-foot privacy fencing, stucco or adobe walls—all can keep young visitors out of harm's way. However, before building a fence, check your local building codes. Your community may require a certain type of fencing.

DEPTH

By controlling the depth of your water garden, keeping it to an inch or less, you can

improve its safety. Consider constructing a shallow reflecting pool, a millstone fountain on a mound of river rock, or a shallow stream. Fill fountains and tub gardens with attractive stones so a child's face cannot be submerged at any point.

HEIGHT

Fountains can be made relatively safe by building the bottom tiers too high for toddlers to tip into; walls should be at least 2½ to 3 feet. Similarly, a wall fountain is a less likely threat if its basin is higher than a toddler's head. Aboveground pools will be similarly safe if you build the sides too tall for small children to climb onto.

EDGING

Every garden pool will have an edge of some material and if it's made of stone, brick, slate, or concrete, it will get slippery, from water or from algae growth.

Edging around an in-ground pool creates a path that beckons children to walk around or balance on. It's better to use turf or edging that blends with surrounding materials to make the contours of the pool less inviting as a play area.

Think carefully before building a shallow beach around a pond. It could prevent small children from falling into deeper sections but might actually entice older, unsupervised children into the water.

PLACEMENT

The placement of your water garden also will affect its safety. Don't locate it just outside the back door; small children can slip out easily and unnoticed and into the water. On the other hand, if you position the pool far away from the house or out of sight, you won't be able to supervise older children.

Consider putting the garden pond in the front yard only if you're absolutely confident neighborhood children won't be attracted to it. Even then, it's advisable to fence it to prevent children from entering. Also, check with your local building-code office first because some communities prohibit front-yard pools.

A water garden by the deck is striking (and an increasingly popular addition), but it could be dangerous in homes where small children live or where they will be frequent visitors. Any deck-side pool should have a railing or fencing surrounding it or the area where it's located.

HINT

For additional safety, install a floating alarm (designed for swimming pools) in your water feature. The alarm will sound if the water surface is disturbed.

The wall of this pool is high enough to keep a toddler from tipping into the water, but older children can climb it. For safety, build walls at least 2½ feet high for toddlers.

A bamboo frame with wire mesh or hardware cloth stapled to the back helps prevent toddlers from falling into this pool. In such an installation, make sure the mesh is strong enough to support the weight of a child and close enough to not trap small feet and hands.

The stones in this small water garden make the water shallow enough that it doesn't pose a threat to wandering children.

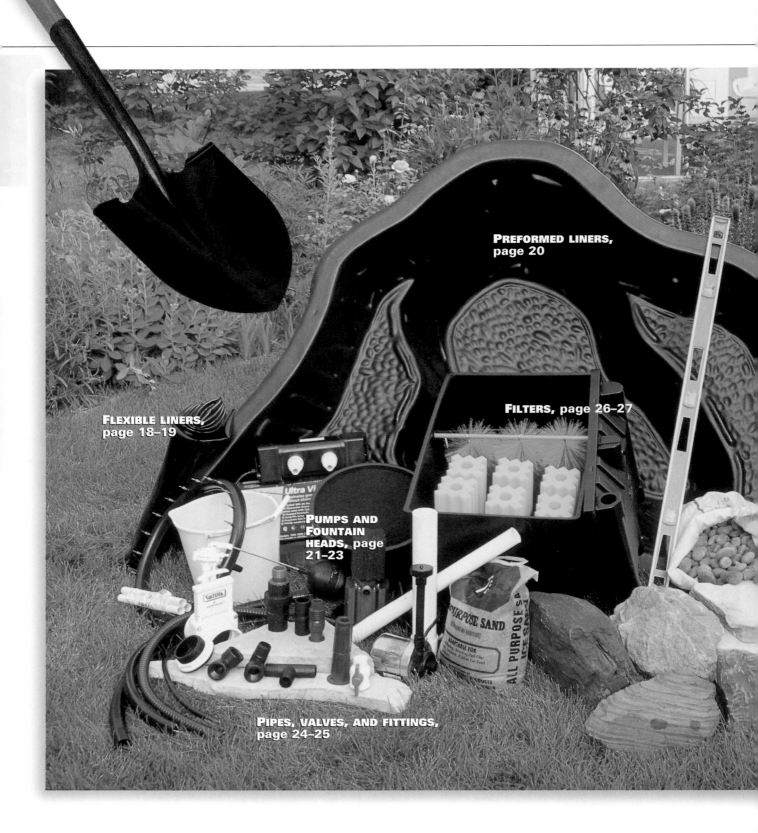

PREFORMED LINERS, page 20

FILTERS, page 26–27

FLEXIBLE LINERS, page 18–19

PUMPS AND FOUNTAIN HEADS, page 21–23

PIPES, VALVES, AND FITTINGS, page 24–25

MATERIALS
AND SUPPLIES

Water gardening has been revolutionized by new materials that make it easier than ever to create a feature that's perfect for your landscape. Not too long ago, creating any kind of water feature meant you had to hire professionals to form and reinforce a concrete water course and install complex plumbing and electrical systems. Today, there's an entirely new way to create water gardens.

Flexible and preformed liners have replaced the concrete, and now you can install most water features yourself—without professional help—in an unending variety of shapes, sizes, and styles.

Pumps install with little effort, use regular household current, and recirculate the water (there's no more need for special plumbing). Fountains attach easily to their supporting structure. Filters (which once had to be installed out of the water) are now often built into the pump. With simplified techniques and equipment, it's possible to install a small water feature in just a weekend.

Although the materials have been revolutionized, the basic tools remain the same. A spade, wheelbarrow, carpenters level, measuring tape, and a pair of heavy leather gloves are the basic tools you'll need to complete your garden pool project.

Make sure all tools are in excellent condition, clean and in good repair, before you begin. Sharpen your spade, tighten the wheelbarrow bolts, and inflate its tire.

The proper materials and supplies, after all, will help you avoid problems as you easily execute your project to produce professional-looking results.

EDGING, page 28–29

LEXIBLE LINERS,
age 18–19

Pond-building materials are more varied and easier to find than ever. In the past two decades, the quality of liners, pumps, filters, and supplies has improved dramatically.

FLEXIBLE LINERS

Flexible liner conforms to your one-of-a-kind creation. Piece it together as you go. Here, overlapped sections create a stream bed flowing into a pond.

One of the most important innovations in garden pond technology is flexible liner. Developed in the 1950s to replace poured concrete and other materials, it allows you to create pools, streams, and waterfalls in just about any shape length, and style you can imagine.

Flexible liner will help you build water gardens in places not possible before. Line an aboveground brick garden pool, for example, or waterproof a whiskey barrel half. Make an artificial stream with sand, gravel, and stones arranged on the liner. Restore a leaky concrete pond by draining it and laying liner over the damaged concrete.

Flexible liners are made from a variety of materials—polyethylene, polyvinyl-chloride (PVC), ethylene-propylene-diene-monomer (EPDM)—and they vary greatly in thickness, cost, and quality. Heavier liners will generally be more expensive, more durable and more puncture and tear resistant than lighter weight liners. However, new liner developments combine durability with light weight. As a rule, the more you spend, the more the liner will resist the sun's ultraviolet (UV) rays.

UV light is the constant enemy of liner material (especially polyethylene). It breaks down the chemical bonds in the liner, making it brittle and easy to rip. If you're going to build a garden pond with polyethylene flexible liner, remember to keep the pond filled with water and the liner completely covered so none of it is exposed.

Most liner comes in black, a color well-suited to garden pools. Black is natural-looking and blends with the algae that tends to cover it after a few months (and helps the liner resist UV damage). Black also gives a pool the illusion of greater depth.

Stock sizes for liners start with 5-foot squares and range up to sections 50 by 100 feet or more. You can join pieces with liner tape or seam sealer made specifically for this purpose to create streams and other large features.

When buying a liner, make sure it is made for use with plants and fish. Liners for other uses (swimming pools or roofs, for example) will be toxic to living things.

UNDERLAYMENT

All liners require the installation of an underlayment, a cushion layer of material between the liner and the soil that prevents punctures and tears. Sand is a good choice for the pool bottom and other horizontal surfaces, but can't be laid vertically. Newspaper is acceptable but deteriorates over time. Old carpet and specially made pond under-layment (which resembles sheets of fiberglass insulation) are ideal.

Some new liners are manufactured with an underlayment already attached. They are extremely puncture resistant and should be used over coarse gravel or sharp rock, for example, or in locations where punctures are likely.

If the liner does tear or puncture, it's no cause for alarm. You'll be able to repair it with a patch and solvent cement. However, you'll have to drain the pool first, clean the area, and let it dry so the patch will stick to the liner.

INSTALLING FLEXIBLE LINER

Flexible liner is relatively easy to install. A water gardener can work alone lining a small pool, but spreading liner out evenly in a larger project may require several people.

You'll find that flexible liner comes with one drawback that preformed liners don't have: You won't be able to avoid folds and creases. As you fill the pond, you'll have to neatly tuck the liner—especially if it's made

of less-elastic polyethylene or PVC—into uneven places so the weight of the water won't stress it unevenly and weaken or tear it. This can be difficult to do, but will be easier if you let the liner warm in the sun an hour or two before you start work.

Once flexible liner is in place and the pool partially filled, work the liner into the nooks and crannies of the pond.

COMPARING FLEXIBLE LINER MATERIALS

Liner Material	Cost	Advantages	Disadvantages	Comments
Polyethylene	5 cents per square foot and more.	Inexpensive. Most hardware and home supply outlets carry it.	Low-density polyethylene is acceptably durable, but avoid high-density polyethylene. Either can be stiff in cold weather. Polyethylene is difficult to repair.	Purchase black, not transparent. Lasts only about two years in a pond. Will last indefinitely, however, when used in a bog garden where it's not exposed to sun.
PVC (polyvinyl chloride)	60 cents per square foot and up.	Moderately durable; sometimes carries a 10-year warranty. Widely available.	PVC for swimming pools and roofs can be toxic to fish and plants.	20- to 32-mil thicknesses. PVC-E is an improved version for fish and plants.
EPDM (ethylene-propylene-diene-monomer)	70 cents per square foot and more.	Very durable; usually carries a 20-year warranty. Stays flexible even in cold weather. Very resistant to UV light damage.	More expensive.	Look for EPDM-SF, which is not toxic to fish and plants and is available in 45-mil thickness.
Butyl rubber (synthetic rubber)	80 cents per square foot and more.	Very durable, sometimes lasting up to 50 years. Usually carries a 20-year warranty. Is more elastic than PVC and polyethylene. Stays flexible even in cold weather.	Most expensive. Can be difficult to find.	Generally sold in 30- or 60-mil thicknesses.

PREFORMED LINERS

Easy to install and well suited to small garden ponds, preformed liners (also called rigid liners) come in many ready-made sizes and styles.

Most preformed liners are made of either fiberglass or rigid plastic. Fiberglass is more expensive but lasts longer than rigid plastic. A small 6- by 3-foot fiberglass liner starts at around $300 (compared with $100 for a rigid-plastic liner); large fiberglass liners can cost $900 or more. Properly installed, a fiberglass liner can last as long as 50 years.

Whether fiberglass or plastic, preformed liners are much more durable than flexible liner and are easier to repair if damaged.

Rigid units have another distinct advantage over flexible liner—they make aboveground water gardens easier to install. They're ideal in areas where stony soil or tree roots prevent or hinder excavation. You can place them either entirely above ground or install them at any depth. But don't expect them to support themselves. Aboveground ponds will need a structure built around them.

Although preformed liners are ideal for formal gardens, they also can be made to look very natural. This one, surrounded by stone, has a small stream flowing into it.

In ground, preformed liners are especially practical for paved areas where the edges can be supported. Rigid liners are available in many shapes, both formal and informal. And if the wide variety of ready-made shapes doesn't suit you, shop around for a manufacturer to custom make one for you.

Standard preformed liners also come in a variety of depths; some include shallow ledges for marginal plants and deep zones for fish to overwinter. For large water gardens—those more than 12 feet long—you can purchase preformed liners in sections that you bolt together and seal with marine silicone. Such sectional liners can be hard to find, however, and require considerably more work. It's better to shop around until you find an existing shape that's right for your landscape.

Although you can buy preformed units in different colors, black is usually best for the same reasons as it is for flexible liner: It's neutral and creates the illusion that the pool is deeper than it actually is.

Compared with flexible liners, the installation of rigid units comes with a few caveats. It's critical, for example, that the liner is absolutely level and that you backfill nooks and crevices so the liner doesn't collapse under the weight of the water. Also, you have to be careful about using heavy edging, such as stone. Some preformed liner edges are convex and the weight of stone will crush them. Other edges are designed to bear weight (check with the supplier), but they must be fully supported with backfill.

> **HINT**
>
> A minimum of 2 inches of soil mixed with sand backfilled under and around a preformed pond will help prevent winter cracking and splitting.

Preformed liners take much of the guesswork out of digging and lining a pool or pond.

PUMPS

Still water in a garden pool is beautiful in its own right, of course. But moving water is what adds that splash and sparkle to your water garden. For that, you'll need a pump.

Pumps make streams run, fountains spray, ponds drain, and water recirculate so that waterfalls keep falling. Moving water through a water feature once required complicated plumbing. Today, all you need is a pump. Installation is uncomplicated, taking just minutes to assemble and set in your pond.

A WORD ABOUT WATER

All local water supplies contain some form of chemical disinfectant, usually chlorine or chloramines. (Chloramines also occur in water naturally.) These disinfectants may be present alone or in combination.

Technically, plants will not be harmed by these chemicals, but attendant wildlife (snails and frogs, for example) will. It's best to remove the disinfectants in a new pond, even if you don't plan to stock fish.

Before you introduce fish or plants to your garden pond, check with your water supplier to see which disinfectants are present in your local water. Then take the following steps to remove them.

Use a dechlorinator to remove chlorine, or let the water in your pond stand for five–seven days (the chlorine will dissipate in this period).

Chloramines will need to be eliminated with a chloramine remover, which also takes out any chlorine present. You can purchase chloramine remover at a water garden supply house. The action of both dechlorinators and chloramine removers is almost immediate— you can introduce fish into the pool shortly after using either one.

Follow the above steps when stocking new ponds and when refilling the pond with more than 10–20 percent of the water volume.

When topping off the pond (to replace evaporation, for example), you don't need to treat tap water. However, you do need to follow these steps:
■ Place the hose in the bottom of the pond.
■ Add the water slowly, in a trickle, to avoid shocking the fish and to prevent them from being attracted to the activity of the water bubbles. (Do not use the hose to aerate ponds containing fish.)
■ Replace *no more* than 10–20 percent of the water at a time, set a timer if necessary.

SUBMERSIBLE OR EXTERNAL?

Pumps are available in submersible and external models, and in both, the mechanism is simply a set of whirling blades that pressurize the water and force it into motion. Submersible pumps are easier to use than external pumps. They sit directly in the water, and unlike external pumps, which you'll have to locate outside the pond, submersibles are inexpensive. They're easy to install, start without priming and run quietly. Submersible pumps can be used for all but the largest water features.

Before buying a pump for your garden pool, check its energy efficiency rating. Large water features require more pump capacity, so they consume more electric energy.

Look for magnetic-driven pumps, which use less energy than direct-driven pumps. (Be forewarned—generally, the most efficient pumps are also the most expensive, but they can pay for themselves in energy efficiency.)

PUMP SIZE

The most important aspect when choosing which pump to buy is getting the right size. Equipment manufacturers rate electrical power in amps or watts, but the critical measure of pump power is the number of gallons of water it will pump per hour to a specific height, called the head.

HINT

Here's an easy way to calculate the volume of your garden pond after you've dug and lined it. Jot down the reading on your water meter. Then fill the garden pond and note the new reading. Most tell you the amount of water used in cubic feet. Convert it to gallons by multiplying by 7.48.

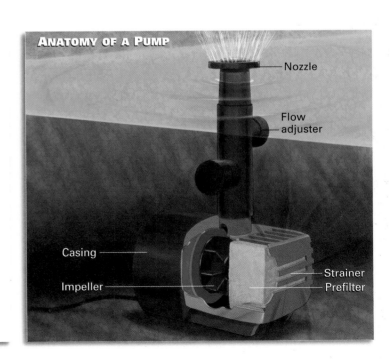

ANATOMY OF A PUMP

Nozzle

Flow adjuster

Casing

Impeller

Strainer

Prefilter

PUMPS
continued

FIGURING THE VOLUME OF FIVE DIFFERENT POOL SHAPES

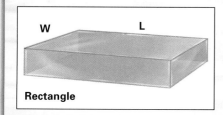

Rectangle

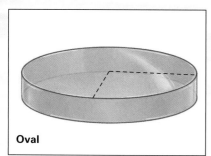

Oval

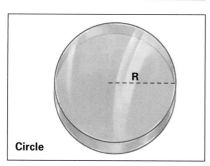

Circle

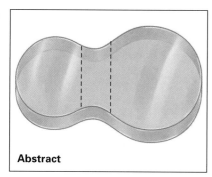

Abstract

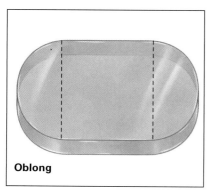

Oblong

For all shapes, the dimensions should be in feet. After calculating the area of the pond, multiply the result by the average depth of the pool. Then multiply that result by 7.48 to get volume in gallons.

RECTANGLE OR SQUARE:
■ *Multiply length by width to find area.*

OVAL:
■ *Measure from center to most distant edge, then from center to nearest edge. Multiply the first figure by the second and the result by 3.14 to find area.*

CIRCLE:
■ *Measure the radius (the length in feet from center to the edge).*
■ *Multiply the radius by itself and then by 3.14 to get area.*

ABSTRACT, IRREGULAR, AND OBLONG:
■ *Break abstract and irregular shapes into simpler units (here, two circles and a rectangle), then calculate the area of each. If that doesn't work, multiply the maximum length by the maximum width to find the pool's area.*
■ *For an oblong, figure the area by breaking it into a square and two half circles. Calculate the area of the square. Then consider the two half circles as one and calculate its area.*

To determine the size pump you'll need, first calculate the volume of water in the pond (see the box at left). As a rule of thumb, choose a pump that can move half the total volume in an hour. For example, if your pond will hold 500 gallons of water, buy a pump that delivers at least 250 gallons an hour.

If your water garden will include a waterfall or stream, it will need a more powerful pump. Pumps have to work harder to move water up a slope or to the head of the stream. (If you're installing a filter as well, you may need to install a separate pump for it.) Figuring exactly how much more power you'll need is somewhat more complicated. In general, the pump should be able to turn over the total volume of water in an hour.

There's an alternate way to determine pump size for a pond with waterfalls. First, measure the width (in inches) of all spillways. For a light, ¼-inch-deep sheet of water going over the falls, figure 50 gallons per hour for each inch of width. For example, if you have three waterfalls that are each 8 inches wide, you'd need a pump that can move at least 1,200 gallons per hour (400 gallons for each of three falls). For a heavier, 1-inch-deep flow, figure 150 gallons per hour per inch of width.

When in doubt, buy a more powerful pump. You can restrict flow with the valve (either self contained or one installed expressly for this purpose). Also, when shopping for a pump for a stream or waterfall, make sure its head or lift is well above the height you've planned for your falls.

OTHER CONSIDERATIONS

Buy the best quality pump you can afford. Pumps with plastic housings are the least expensive and least durable. Brass, bronze, and stainless steel housings last longer. Aluminum housings will eventually corrode.

Pumps have varying lengths of cord; check to make sure the cord is long enough to go through the pond and plug in well away from the water. The longer the better, especially since some codes specify that the electrical outlet for a water feature has to be at least 6 feet away from water. Avoid extension cords if possible (see precautions on page 43). If you have to use one, make sure it's made for outdoor use and is plugged into a ground fault interrupter (GFI), a device that shuts off an outlet immediately if there is an overload.

Some pumps come equipped with prefilters. If you need a filter, you can determine what type by referring to page 26.

Finally, be sure to buy a pump that is designed for use in a water garden. Unlike other types of pumps, those for water gardens sustain continuous, round-the-clock use.

FOUNTAIN HEADS

The most popular use for a pump is to power a fountain, and there are more choices in fountain spray patterns than ever before—one for just about any garden style.

A fountain head—also called a spray head—is usually sold separately from the pump (although some pumps include them). When choosing a fountain head, first consider the height and width of its spray pattern, although you can often adjust both with a valve on the pump. Second, choose the style that fits the appearance of your water feature. A bubbler, for example, looks natural in a small,

informal water garden tucked into a perennial border or among shrubs. A mushroom or bell is striking in a circular formal pool. And a rotating jet adds dazzle to a starkly modern installation.

Fountains, especially geysers or bubblers, also aerate the water for fish—an added benefit. However, you may have to consider the needs of plants. Many, including water lilies, don't like water on their leaves and prefer an undisturbed surface.

Fountains with delicate or tall sprays need some shelter; strong winds distort the pattern, increase evaporation, and deplete the pool.

Bell or mushroom

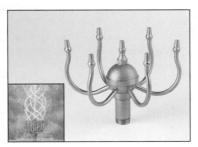

Rotating jet

Bubbler

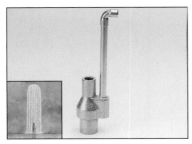

Geyser

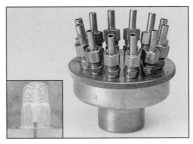

One-tier spray

Multi-tier spray

Flower, tulip, or trumpet spray

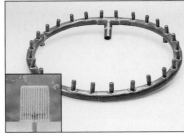

Fountain ring

Fleur-de-lis

Poolside ornament

In-pool fountain ornament

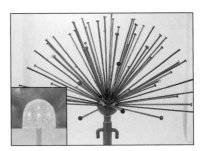

Hemisphere

PIPES, VALVES, AND FITTINGS

Although not as glamorous as colorful water lilies or glittering fish, pipes, valves, and fittings are the workhorses of your garden pond. They're readily available at most hardware stores (or from water garden suppliers), but choose them with care. The right pipes, valves, and fittings can dramatically improve the efficiency of your pump.

Buy smooth-bore pipe (instead of pipe that's ridged inside) to reduce water friction and speed its flow. Plan piping to minimize elbows and sharp bends, which slow the water flow.

The following primer will help you choose the right piping and supplies for your garden pond.

PIPES: Pipes deliver water where you want it, and they protect underground electric lines from deterioration or cuts from a wayward spade or other tool.

Although copper might seem like the best choice for carrying water, plastic is actually better in garden ponds. Unlike copper and some other metals, plastic isn't toxic to plants and fish. It is easy to cut, simple to assemble, and it won't corrode. Where your plan calls for nonflexible pipe, look for rigid PVC with a schedule-40 pressure rating. For other applications, use flexible corrugated plastic pipe. It bends around corners and other obstacles without using additional fittings. (It won't, however, make sharp 90-degree angles without an elbow.)

In most garden ponds, ½-inch to 1¼-inch pipe and fittings will do the job. If your project requires moving large amounts of water, use 1½- to 2-inch pipe.

FITTINGS: Fittings are the joints of the water-supply system. They connect the parts, pumps, pipes, and filters. If you want your pump to run both a waterfall and a fountain, for example, you can put a fitting on it to pump just the fountain, just the waterfall, or both at the same time. Other fittings allow you to make the liner watertight where piping passes through it. There are three types of fittings.

■ **SOLVENT FITTINGS,** also called slip fittings, require a solvent to join them together. They are more complicated to use than other fittings. Use them with rigid PVC pipe. All surfaces need to be clean and dry before applying solvent to the pipe.

■ **THREADED FITTINGS,** those that screw into place, are easy to install, even when wet. Use them primarily with rigid pipes. Make threaded fittings waterproof by winding pipe-wrap tape around the threads before assembling.

■ **BARBED** (also called push-in or compression) fittings just push together. They're used with most kinds of flexible pipe and need a stainless steel or plastic clamp to keep them secure. They're inexpensive and simple to install.

VALVES: Valves control and divert the flow of water. You can use a valve to shut off the water supply, or to adjust the rate of water flow, split a water source to two or even three separate lines and outlets, or use it to open up a line to drain the garden pool.

HINT

When shopping for plumbing supplies, take along a sketch of your plans so the supplier can help you find the least expensive and most effective setup.

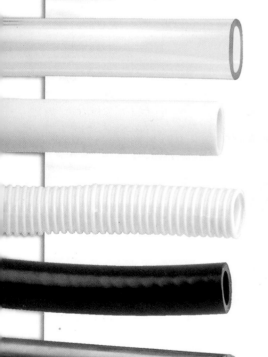

PIPES

Clear vinyl tubing: Easy to see through but clogs and kinks very quickly; it is best used only where short lengths are needed.

Rigid PVC: Use schedule-40 pressure-rated pipe and fittings. It is corrosion resistant, lightweight, and inexpensive, but not flexible. Commonly available in white but can be spray-painted black where it's visible underwater.

Corrugated plastic: Extremely flexible, which makes it especially useful for water gardens. Can be expensive and requires barbed fittings with clamps.

Black plastic: Many brands and styles. Semiflexible, inexpensive, and requires barbed fittings and clamps. Good pipe to bury underground; and, because it's flexible, requires fewer elbows.

Metal: Copper or galvanized steel. Can be toxic to some pond life, such as snails and dragonfly larvae. Expensive and not recommended.

FITTINGS

Reducer: *Allows you to change from one size pipe to another. Larger pipe moves more water faster because it creates less back pressure and less friction.*

Adapter: *Used to join two different types of pipe or two different fittings, such as a solvent and a threaded fitting.*

T-piece: *Joins three pieces of pipe. Often used in a pump line to move water to both a waterfall and a fountain.*

Coupler: *Used to join two pieces of pipe of the same size into one longer piece.*

Elbow: *Changes the direction of a pipe and the water flow. Available in 90- and 45-degree turns. To reduce friction, use two 45-degree elbows instead of one 90-degree elbow.*

Bulkhead: *Attaches to the side of a water feature. Allows pipe to pass through the liner or wall without leakage. Not available as a barbed fitting.*

VALVES

Ball valve: *Best used to turn water flow off and on quickly. Not as useful for fine-tuning the flow.*

Gate valve: *Use to restrict or increase flow. Minor adjustments are easy to make. Can be used as an on-off valve but is slower to operate than a ball valve.*

Check or one-way valve: *Keeps water flowing in just one direction, ideal where you need to prevent backflow. Useful when power fails or is shut off to the water pump.*

Two-way valve: *Allows you to do several things with the same valve: Shut off the water, control the flow to a fountain head, or open up a line to drain the pool.*

Float valve: *Turns water off and on depending on the water level in the water feature. Reduces the chore of adding water during hot weather.*

FILTERS

Filters come in all shapes, sizes, and styles. From left: a biological filter, a prefilter with foam inside a rigid casing, and an all-foam prefilter. A UV clarifier is in the foreground.

A filter—if you need one—has a big job to do. It will keep water clear and prevent your pumps from clogging with water-garden debris—fish waste, decayed organic matter, floating algae, leftover fish food, and many other unwanted tiny particles.

Not every garden pond that's home to both fish and plants will need a filter because a well-balanced ecosystem usually "cleans" itself sufficiently. If you can tolerate water that's less than clear, so can the plants and fish. But if the garden pond you are planning will be home to fish and not to plants, you'll have to install a filter to clean up after the fish.

The type of filter or filters—many gardeners use a combination—you'll need depends both on your tolerance for murky water and on the type of water feature you have. A wildlife pond should have a little algae, but water splashing in a white marble fountain must be crystal clear.

After planning the design of your water feature, consult with your water garden supplier to learn which of the following filters is best for your installation.

TYPES OF FILTERS

MECHANICAL FILTERS: Using any one of a variety of materials—foam, screens, mesh, or brushes—mechanical filters strain and trap dirt and debris. The simplest form of mechanical filter is a screen on the inlet side

of the pump. More complex and larger units are sold separately. Most prefilters (those installed between the water source and the pump to keep larger debris from clogging the pump) are mechanical.

Mechanical filters are reasonably priced, but they clog easily, especially in heavy service, in ponds containing many fish and plants, or in undersized ponds. You'll need to spend at least a few minutes weekly (and possibly daily in the summer) cleaning them.

You can outfit a large pond with a high-rate sand filter, like those used in swimming pools, however, these are rarely recommended any more. They are large, noisy and require a powerful pump with extensive plumbing.

BIOLOGICAL FILTERS: Biological filters are similar to mechanical filters, but instead of strainers, their filter beds contain live bacteria, which break down toxic ammonia and other harmful substances. In this process, the bacteria convert ammonia compounds first into nitrites, then into nitrates, which plants use in their growth. It takes a few weeks in spring for the bacteria colonies to grow large enough to be effective filters.

Clean biological filters every month or two by rinsing off one-fourth to one-third of their elements. If you clean any more than that, you remove too much bacteria from the elements and end up with a "starter" filter, one requiring several weeks for the bacteria to build back up to effective levels.

ANATOMY OF A COMBINATION MECHANICAL-BIOLOGICAL FILTER

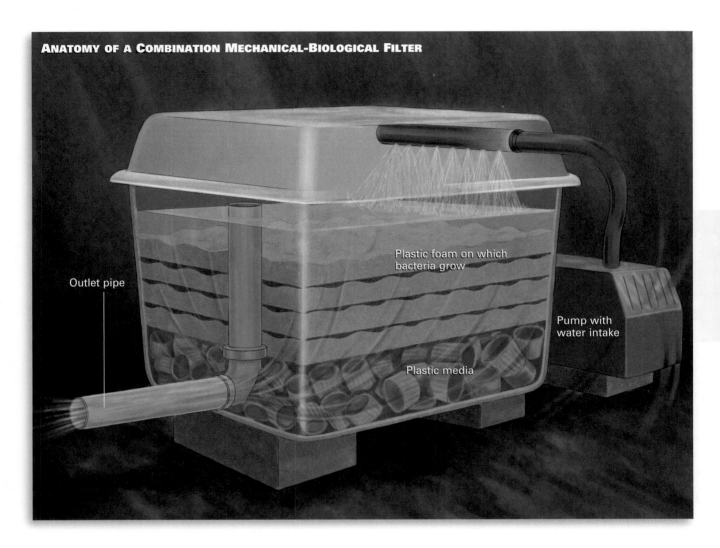

Outlet pipe

Plastic foam on which bacteria grow

Pump with water intake

Plastic media

In a small pond, you can use an in-pond filter. Large ponds, however, may require large unsightly tanks that sit alongside the pond.

CHEMICAL FILTERS: As the name implies, these filters remove impurities in the water through chemical action. The pond water is circulated through activated carbon or a mineral called zeolite. Chemical filters are often combined with biological filters.

VEGGIE FILTERS: Using nature's own water purifying abilities, a veggie filter is actually a small plant-filled pond or tub connected to the main pond. The plants consume surplus nutrients, reducing algae growth in the main pond. A tub veggie filter can be rigged so that water flows into the tub, through the roots, and back to the main pond. Garden ponds with a significant number of plants won't benefit from a veggie filter because the existing plants do the filtering themselves.

UV CLARIFIERS OR STERILIZERS: The high-tech solution to cloudy water, these are often used as companions to biological and mechanical filters. They consist of an ultraviolet bulb encased in a clear waterproof casing. When algae, bacteria, viruses, and certain fish parasites are exposed to the UV light, they die. The light also encourages organic particles to clump together, which makes it easier for a mechanical filter to trap them.

HINT

Make your own inexpensive prefilter by placing the pump in a large water lily planting basket (the kind with an open weave). Then fill the basket with sand-free pea gravel.

FILTER SIZE

Pond water is pushed (or pulled) through the filter by your pump, and the size of the filter has to match both the volume of your garden pool and the power of your pump. Before you purchase a filter, calculate the capacity of your water feature (see page 22). Then check the filter specifications and make sure it can handle the amount of water your pump exchanges in an hour.

EDGING

Selecting and installing the right edging for your water garden is critical. Edging not only hides the liner, it also defines the style of your garden pond and sets its mood.

Rough boulders, especially native stone, look just right around a naturalistic pond or stream. Turf is good for a formal pool set in the middle of a lawn. Brick and cut stone—rectangular or square—lend themselves to formal garden ponds. Flagstone works well in informal water gardens.

Select edging with a character compatible with the materials or landscape that surround the pool. Flagstone works best when there is similar stone in the landscape. Brick is attractive in a garden pool set near a brick house or patio.

You might edge the pond with hardscape, cutting it into or locating it adjacent to a deck or patio, for example. Such installations are easiest to create when designed from the ground up with the deck or patio, but most existing structures can be retrofitted with a water feature of some kind. Before you choose edging, consider the following aspects of its use, cost, and installation.

TURF

Turf makes a striking edging for formal pools set in a flat stretch of lawn. It is a good choice to use around in-ground preformed liners that can't support much weight. The site for a turf-edged pond should be flat (or made so by filling in with soil) because on slopes, water in the pond levels out, exposing the liner on the upper slope.

Use turf as edging only when you can keep the surrounding lawn in excellent health. But take great care when applying fertilizer and pesticides around the water feature. Although these materials don't usually run off turf, the spreader can fling them into the water. Nitrogen and phosphorus in the fertilizer can promote growth of algae in the pond. And fish are highly sensitive to many pesticides, including some organic ones.

It costs little to install a turf edging. And installation is easy—pat soil over the liner edge and toss some seed on it. Installing sod requires a little more effort but is worth it—sod keeps soil from eroding into the pond.

A turf edging takes care. The shallow rooting area means roots burn easily. So don't let the grass dry out. Keep clippings out of the water when you mow. Hand trim around the pond every week or so.

FLAGSTONE

Flagstone combines well with boulders, gravel, sand, or rock in naturalistic settings. It's easy to install as an edging and ideal for a variety of water features—including ones on slopes—because you can stack it. It is excellent for securing flexible liner in place and it can be mortared for stability and permanence.

Limestone is the most popular flagstone. Its appearance improves as it weathers and as moss and algae grow on it.

To use flagstone, dig a shallow shelf around the pool. Experiment with placing the pieces so they fit together neatly. Cut large stones with a circular saw that has a masonry blade, or rent a stone-cutting saw. Local stone is the least expensive (about $1 a square foot or less) and often the most natural looking.

BRICK AND CONCRETE PAVERS

Brick and concrete pavers make great extensions of materials used in patios, walks, or other hardscape. Depending on the method you use, brick and concrete pavers can be easy to install or a challenge. It's fairly easy to lay them dry in sand, for example, but more difficult to set them in concrete.

Mortared brick and pavers have advantages over those set dry. First, you can cantilever them over the water to minimize the amount of exposed liner. Second, mortar won't erode into the pond like sand, dirt, and other dry construction materials will.

CUT STONE

More expensive and more formal than flagstone in appearance, cut stone looks most appropriate around square or rectangular pools. Excellent in most formal gardens, it blends well (depending on its color) with gravel, wood, and brick, as well as a number of other materials.

Cut stone is challenging to work with—its right-angled edges must fit perfectly, and it needs to be mortared in place. Cut stone is excellent for cantilevering to conceal the liner. Choose stone with a rough surface so that it won't be too slippery when wet.

BOULDERS

Ideal for naturalistic ponds, small boulders are relatively easy to work with. You'll need help to move any large boulders you install, and unless you find a free supply, their purchase price and delivery costs will be high.

Boulders work well set in sand or gravel, although you can mortar them for permanence. Most boulders should be buried to one-third or one-half of their diameter for a natural effect. They are striking combined with cut stone and flagstone.

PATIOS AND DECKING

Water features built into a patio or deck put the water at a level where it's easy to enjoy, and such designs are increasing in popularity. You should install them when you build the deck or patio, of course. However, garden ponds are an easy retrofit—especially to a deck. Cut them directly into the existing structure or set them adjacent to it.

You won't have to buy separate edging material for the pond, so a deck or patio addition will be relatively inexpensive. Make sure that the wood has not been treated with preservatives that can leach into the water and harm plants or fish. Especially avoid pentachlorophenol- or creosote-treated wood. And if you're thinking about using redwood, you'll need to season it for at least a year or until it turns gray. Fresh redwood contains toxic tannins.

BUILDING A GARDEN POOL

Building a garden pond or other water feature is not a difficult task—even for beginners. You can read the instructions presented in this chapter and proceed with confidence, no matter what style water feature you've chosen. If you have a few basic home gardening tools, you're already well armed for the work, and, with two exceptions—electrical work and excavation of large projects—you probably won't have to hire an outside contractor.

Electrical work and excavation will be the most daunting parts of the project. Although it's advisable for safety's sake—and may be required by city building code—to hire out most electrical work to a licensed electrician and to contract large-scale excavations, you still need to educate yourself on the basics. Then, you'll be able talk more knowledgeably with the contractor, if you hire one.

Excavating even a small installation can be a chore—or it can remind you of the days when you were 12 years old and digging a big hole was pure fun. The key to whether it's fun or frustrating lies in correctly estimating how much you can do by yourself. Don't overdo it. For unusually large projects, you might need to contract out the work to someone with a backhoe. (Or you can rent one, if you have the skills to operate it.)

You can use professionals, of course, for other parts of the project if you want (or absolutely have to). However, you'll spend more and miss out on the fun of building your own water feature.

Garden pool installation, like most home-improvement projects, is easier to accomplish with two people. Whether you're installing flexible liner, leveling a rigid liner, laying stone, hauling away dirt, or just in need of a second opinion, a companion greatly speeds up the project.

And, as you launch into building your garden pond, allow yourself plenty of time for each step. Most homeowners tend to be overly optimistic with their estimates of the time it will take to complete a project. Remember that there are always unexpected complications, unforeseen trips to the hardware store, and many other time-consuming tasks you won't anticipate.

Building a water feature is no small job, but it's an excellent do-it-yourself project. Recent innovations in materials for pool and pond construction make the job even easier. You can complete a small project in a weekend, but larger ones will require more time.

STARTER GARDENS

Even if you want a big water garden with a waterfall, stream, and a variety of fish and plants, make a starter garden first. A small-scale project offers experience you'll find helpful when tackling larger projects later.

A starter garden brings the beauty of water to your landscape in a minimum of time and for much less cost than it takes to develop a large water feature. It is also more manageable when it comes to time, requiring less than an hour of maintenance every few weeks.

You can have a water garden in little more space than this book takes up. Sometimes called mini ponds or mini gardens, starter gardens set by an entrance are a delight for visitors. Tucked into a corner of a patio, they're a pleasant source of sound or a sparkling focal point when incorporated into the landscape.

You can make a mini pond that's formal or informal, raised or in ground. The logical choice for small yards or patios, mini gardens provide a point of interest in a courtyard or in a tiny plot outside an apartment.

Clay pots and pottery shards create a whimsical fountain that takes little time to build or maintain. In cold climates, however, bring such a fountain indoors for the winter.

Urns are popular containers for fountains. And they're easy to set up. Simply install a small pump in the bottom of the urn and fill with water.

HINT

If water becomes cloudy or foul smelling in a small starter water garden, remove 10 percent of the water from the bottom with either a siphon hose or water pump. This reduces the buildup of toxic organic wastes.

HOME- OR FACTORY-MADE

Starter gardens can be handmade or come from the factory ready to install. Make one from a ceramic pot. Or try a small kidney-shaped pond formed with flexible liner and tucked into a flower bed. A premade fountain, outfitted with fish and plants, or an aboveground preformed garden complete with flagstones stacked in a low wall around a liner can serve as a starter garden. There are even portable water gardens.

Starter gardens are an inspiration. Many people who begin small find they've enjoyed their first creation so much that they want to do a second, more ambitious feature, building on the skills they have acquired. Beginning gardens can also provide the first piece of a much larger project. For example, your small pool could eventually become the foot of a waterfall or a stream. Or, it could be the first in a series of pools connected by bridges or pathways.

Your starter garden could be just a temporary one, there until you move on to bigger projects. If you dispose of it, you can reuse the flexible liner and resite flagstones and boulders in the landscape. When finished with a water garden container, you can fill it with soil and use it as a planter. And you can reuse a pump in a new water feature or sell it to another aspiring water gardener.

FISH AND FOUNTAINS

For plants and fish, a mini garden should hold at least 5 gallons of water, but leave out the fountain. A fountain in a container that small splashes too much for fish and plants. Splashing interferes with plant growth and creates currents the fish have to fight. Instead, equip minimum-size gardens with a small poolside spitter fountain or a gentle aquarium bubbler to aerate the water without creating too much disturbance.

CONTAINER WATER GARDENS

Container water gardens are perhaps the easiest starter water garden. You can build a container garden in an hour or two with no

The sounds from Japanese-style water features with bamboo fountains create a pleasant, relaxing atmosphere.

Combining statuary and water into one, this charming small pool is a good choice for a family with small children. The stones make it difficult for a child to be harmed by the amount of water in the bowl.

digging and little expense. And you can locate them in places you may not have considered for a water garden—places unsuitable for any kind of large-scale pond project, such as on a deck.

Virtually any kind of container can be used for a water garden. If it holds water—or can be made to hold water—you can turn it into a water garden. Here are some suggestions: whiskey half-barrels; galvanized buckets or livestock troughs (older ones that are no longer shiny, otherwise they can be toxic); oversized dishes or bowls; boulders or rocks with hollows; black plastic tubs designed for water gardens; wooden buckets; iron kettles; claw-foot bathtubs; even rubber boots.

Small water features are ideal for tucking into plantings, making the pool seem as though it emerged from the earth. The effect is doubled as the rim becomes covered with moss.

Small size doesn't preclude beauty. This water lily is stunning in a blue ceramic container.

STARTER GARDENS
continued

Try using an item you can fully or partially sink into the ground, depending on your location. In-ground locations help minimize summer temperature fluctuations. You especially want to sink unattractive plastic containers, such as buckets and dishpans, into the ground up to their lip, then disguise them with plants and stones.

If you're planning to have fish and simply must have an aboveground starter garden, locate it in a spot that receives afternoon shade during the summer.

IS IT WATERPROOF?

After choosing your container, check it for watertightness. Place it on a nonporous, dry surface, such as a sidewalk or driveway, then fill it with water. Let it sit for a day, checking occasionally for leaks. If it leaks, seal minor cracks from the inside with aquarium sealant.

You can make porous containers watertight by painting them with a rubberized sealant available from water garden suppliers, with swimming pool paint, or flexible liner. (Whiskey-barrel halves must be lined to keep impurities in the wood from killing fish.) If you use flexible liner, tuck it carefully into all recesses inside the container, then staple or glue the liner's edges to the container with aquarium sealant.

To add a fountain to a container water garden, drill a hole in the container, if it has no drainage hole. Next, cut a small patch of flexible liner, punch a hole in it and thread the electrical cord for the pump through it and out of the pot. Spread caulk or sealant over the patch and attach the patch to the container (the caulk acts as an adhesive). The caulk must be labeled for use underwater. After installing the pump, pull excess cord out of the container through the hole in the patch and caulk around the cord at the patch to tightly seal the pot.

STARTER FEATURES

PLANTS: Choose plants for your container in keeping with its scale. Miniature water lilies, fairy moss (*Azolla caroliniana*), miniature cattail (*Typha minima*), water-loving iris (such as *Iris laevigata*), or whirly-stemmed rush (*Juncus effusus* 'Spiralis') are naturals for growing in container water gardens. Plants that trail over edges, such as parrot's feather (*Myriophyllum aquaticum*) with its feathery leaves and curling stems, also work well.

FISH: If you'll be stocking your mini pond, you'll need to balance plant needs for sun with fish needs for oxygen. Most water garden plants do best with six or more hours of full sun. That much sun on a hot day can heat up the water significantly. In turn, the water becomes oxygen depleted, which stresses the fish. However, you can help fish get enough oxygen even in a warm site by positioning your starter garden where it receives afternoon shade. Keep a thermometer in the water, and never let the water get warmer than 85° F. If fish surface to gasp for air, aerate the water immediately. You can use a small battery-powered aeration pump or an air stone, a device connected to a small external pump and placed in the pool.

Also, because your starter garden will hold only a few fish, you'll need to control the population by relocating offspring.

Among the easiest and least expensive of all water features, a container water garden fits in beautifully when tucked among other container plantings.

HINT

Copper containers are toxic to fish and other aquatic animals. They should not be used for water garden containers unless lined with another material.

FOUNTAINS: A charming addition to a water garden, a fountain also helps to oxygenate the water. The fountain head and volume have to be just right, however, in container water gardens. Avoid large, high sprays; choose a spray pattern that is in keeping with the container style. Remember, too, that most floating plants don't like their leaves splashed, and if the container is very small you should choose between having fish and plants or a fountain.

You'll need only the smallest of pumps—a bubbler is a good choice—and it should allow you to adjust the fountain spray to the right size for the container garden. Hide the electrical cord among plants, or bury it under gravel.

WINTER CARE

You can leave container water gardens outdoors in winter in mild climates where average temperatures stay above 20° F. In these mild areas, you can sink the container into the ground, leaving only an inch or two of it visible, and this will sufficiently insulate the container from temperature fluctuations.

In colder climates where average winter temperatures fall to minus 10° F or below, bring container water gardens—especially ones made from breakable materials such as terra-cotta and ceramic—indoors. Also drain starter water gardens that are installed in the ground. Otherwise they will crack.

CREATING A CONTAINER WATER GARDEN

1. SEAL: Any container that you can waterproof can be turned into a water garden. Plug drainage holes with a rubber-gasketed stainless steel bolt or a piece of liner spread with caulk. Seal any minor cracks with caulk or brush on water garden sealant. Use flexible liner to waterproof wooden and other leaky containers.

2. INSTALL THE PUMP: To grow fish and plants, add an aquarium bubbler or small spitter fountain to oxygenate water. To determine pump size, measure the container volume by filling it from 5-gallon buckets. Conceal the cord, and plug it into a GFI outlet.

3. FILL: Fill the container with water. Before planting or stocking with fish, let the water sit for five to seven days to dissipate chlorine and stabilize the water temperature. Or add a chloramine remover (refer to page 21 before beginning this process).

4. PLANT: Plants act as natural filters to keep the water clear. Choose plants with a variety of shapes, textures, and colors. Include some that will dangle over the edge and others, such as grasses or sedges, that are tall and spiky. You may need to set the smaller pots on bricks to raise them to the correct depth.

5. ADD FISH: Fish make an ordinary water garden extraordinary. Allow them to adjust gradually to the water temperature by leaving them in their original water in a plastic bag. Tie the bag and let it float in the container water. After ten minutes, release the fish. Feed them only occasionally; overfeeding can kill them.

POSITIONING:
ENVIRONMENTAL CONSIDERATIONS

Where you place a water feature is almost as important as what type of feature you choose.

Position it well and you'll have thriving, healthy fish, plants that bloom and grow happily, clear water, and minimal maintenance.

Position it badly and you'll risk diseases of fish and plants, green water, and maintenance problems.

When deciding where to position your water garden, consider the following points.

SUN: If you want plants, pick a site receiving at least four to six hours of direct sunlight daily. Most water plants grow in sunny locations. Avoid sun-baked sites, however. They heat the water, which speeds evaporation and kills fish. You can enliven shady spots with a water feature, turning them into cool havens on hot summer days. However, because few plants thrive in full shade, choose a water feature without plants.

TREES: As a rule, you should locate your water feature away from tall plants and trees (consider their mature height, not their present height). Tall plants cast too much shade, and trees drop leaves and seeds that can pollute the water (or, like yews and walnuts, can poison it). Tree roots can present excavation problems and damage water garden liners.

HINT

Once you've had utility companies mark the layout of their lines, draw a map of your property and mark the lines for reference in future landscaping projects.

This water garden is ideally sited in full sun, which supports the widest variety of plants and fish. It's also close enough to the house to afford easy electrical access to power pumps, filters, and lights.

ELEVATION: Low spots might seem ideal for a water feature, but remember that they collect runoff from lawns and are prone to flooding. Low spots also make a garden pond hard to drain without a pump and are pockets for frost and early freezes. If you must put your water feature in such a location, build a berm or other barrier to prevent too much water from flowing into it.

On the other hand, a sloping site—even one that rises or drops off sharply—is perfect for certain water features. Retaining walls and terraces can serve as the foundation for striking garden-pond designs. Slopes also provide perfect sites for a waterfall or a series of them.

WIND: Position your garden pond so it's sheltered from the wind. Wind can distort the pattern of a fountain, damage the succulent stems of bog plants, and harm floating plants that need tranquil water. It also speeds the evaporation of water. If wind is an unavoidable problem, consider erecting a hedge, screen, or fence with gaps, such as trelliswork. (A solid fence can actually increase wind flow by funneling it over and down.)

UTILITY ACCESS: Locate your water feature near a readily available water source. You'll be topping off your pond more often

Not only is this water garden close to a sitting area for regular enjoyment, it's also in a sheltered site that prevents premature freezing and plant damage.

If your garden is already shaping up informally with naturalistic plantings, then a pond such as this one would blend in nicely. The rough stone edging and undulating shape make it seem as though it's always been there.

in hot weather and cleaning it out occasionally with spray from a hose. Also, site the pond near an existing outlet if your plan includes electrical features. You can run a line and freestanding GFI outlet to the water feature, but that can be expensive.

REFLECTION: One of the delights of water features is that they reflect what's above or next to them, such as open sky or a lovely flower bed. However, if they're positioned near a utility pole or another eyesore, you will simply double an unattractive view. To see exactly what your water garden will reflect, lay a large mirror on the spot, if possible, to check the reflected view. This will also help you observe the direction and quality of reflected light at different times of the day.

EXISTING LANDSCAPE FEATURES: Site your garden pond several feet away from fences, buildings, and other landscape features so you'll have room to maintain it from all sides and so the pond doesn't create moisture problems for buried posts or foundations.

You will also need to leave several feet (most local building codes require a 5-foot clearance) between the site and any fences and buildings to prevent construction problems.

WATER TABLE: If you live in an area with a high water table, you'll want to position your water feature on an elevated site. Rising water tables can push the liner out of the ground,

DEALING WITH UTILITY LINES

When planning an in-ground water feature, call the phone, cable, gas, and electrical companies and ask them to mark buried lines so you can avoid digging in those locations. It is extremely dangerous to cut through a utility line with a spade or backhoe, and can also be embarrassing if you cut off power to your neighborhood or break a gas line.

Locate a garden pond away from utility lines so your site won't cause future utility maintenance problems. Don't place an aboveground feature over buried lines.

If utility lines interfere significantly with your plans, your utility company may be willing to move them. Some companies don't charge for this service.

distorting and damaging it. Do a little advance work in the spring. That's when water levels are likely to be their highest. Determine your water level by digging a narrow hole 3 feet deep. Cover it with waterproof plastic—to divert rain—and a piece of thick scrap wood to prevent someone from stepping into the hole. Check it over a two- to three-week period to see if the water level has risen.

This water feature, while lovely, is likely to have problems because trees constantly drop litter. Avoiding roots is difficult when excavating a large water feature near mature trees.

Pay attention to what's overhead. Make sure your pond or stream is well-positioned for reflecting the sky. Look for power lines, dead tree branches, and any other unsightly object that can become magnified when seen in a still pool of water.

POSITIONING: DESIGN CONSIDERATIONS

Use a water feature to direct garden traffic. This stream and bridge draw people and encourage them to stroll into the back part of the landscape where they might not otherwise go.

Garden pools, more than most other landscape elements you will consider, must fit perfectly into the overall layout. After all, a water feature is likely to be one of the highlights of your landscape. Find the best site to get the most out of your pool.

USES AND VIEWS

One of the first things to consider when positioning your water feature is how you'll use it. Do you desire something cool and splashing to enjoy while sitting on your patio or deck? Then you'll want the pond close by. Or, maybe you're envisioning a lovely formal pool that will serve as the focal point of the overall landscape. That means you'll be positioning it at a distance so you can view it with the landscape as a whole. Perhaps you want to create a highly naturalistic wildlife habitat. That suggests a location in a less-used part of your property where it won't matter if things get a little wild and overgrown and where humans won't continually scare off animal visitors.

A water feature should always work integrally into the landscape—never just plunked into the middle of a lawn, isolated from everything else. The most successfully designed water features are usually attached to another part of the landscape—a flower bed, a deck, a patio. Garden ponds are part of the design, not just add-ons.

One way to make a water garden seem like it's always been there is to study the contours of your land. Even seemingly flat sites have slight rises and slopes. Although you don't want to put your water garden in a very low spot, you might want it to hug a curve at the bottom of a slight slope for a natural look.

Sometimes a water garden will fit logically into the lines and contours of your landscape—tucked into a flower bed or set in a just-perfect spot next to a deck.

Ponds and pools are ideal for positioning next to a deck or patio where their beauty can be enjoyed up close. This aboveground pool brings the water nearly to eye level for people sitting on the bench.

ELEVATION AND SURROUNDINGS

Consider, too, from what elevation you'll be viewing the water feature. If you'll be seeing it from some distance, it's ideal to locate it so you look at least slightly down upon it. If the pond will be near a seating area, it's pleasant to have it close to chest level (when seated)—to invite dangling fingers in the cool water or view the goldfish up close. Locating a water garden so you have to look up to view it is seldom a good idea.

As much as possible, "steal" from the neighboring landscape. If you (or your neighbor) has an especially lovely large tree, for example, it makes sense to put the water garden where it can reflect some of the spring or fall color. Or, use your garden pond to underline a pretty view into an adjacent field or mark the entrance into a woods.

When well-designed, water features offer an opportunity to make your landscape feel bigger. Run a rectangular pool with the long side parallel to your main view from the house to make the yard seem longer. A triangular pool with its base pointing to the far end of the yard exaggerates the perspective and makes the landscape appear larger.

Smaller pools also add unexpected interest for visitors who happen upon them. Consider tucking a small pond into a side yard or around the bend of a curving flower bed, suggesting that the landscape is packed with surprises if the visitors keep looking. Include space for a bench or outdoor chairs—a perfect location to enjoy your pond.

It makes sense—a formal pool for a formal garden. This round pool is a novel focal point in an herb garden. Water gardens and herbs combine well because both do best in full sun.

Even in dreary weather, these homeowners can enjoy their pond. Located just outside the door, it offers a perfect second-story view.

Wherever you place your water feature, "test drive" its position by marking its outline with a garden hose, rope, garden lime, or white flour. Live with the stand-in for a week or so. This will help you decide if the new position capitalizes on views from the house, patio, and other spots on your property. (View the marked-in garden from every window in your house.) This trial run will also ensure that the water feature fits in with existing traffic patterns in your landscape and leaves enough space for outdoor furniture and other objects. Check, too, how much light the test site gets and take note of the wind in that area.

Water gardens are most attractive when viewed from above. You can look down slightly on this garden and appreciate how its curving lines echo the curves of the flower beds and borders.

DEPTH

The depth of your water garden depends on a number of factors—its size, what fish, wildlife, and plants you will use, and what type of soil you have. Although most garden ponds may look deep, even large water features are often no deeper than 2 feet. That's good news for do-it-yourselfers—and their backs. However, the deeper the pond, the easier it is to stabilize its temperature. Except in the coldest climates, a pond 24 inches deep usually won't freeze solid, killing fish and damaging rigid liner.

Deeper ponds also stay cooler in summer. Small, shallow ponds, less than 18 inches deep, heat up quickly, depleting oxygen and stressing fish and possibly killing them. Shallow water features also are more subject to excess algae growth during hot weather.

Small ponds, those with a surface of 5 to 10 square feet, can be as shallow as 12 inches (a depth of 18 inches is preferred). Pools with 50 to 500 square feet should be between 18 and 36 inches deep. Large ponds, those of 500 square feet or more, can be up to 5 feet deep.

To some extent, the depth of your pond may be dictated by soil type. Stony soil or soil with hardpan (a difficult-to-penetrate crust a few to many inches beneath the surface) may limit the depth you can dig. Tree roots, too, may keep you from making a pond as deep as you'd like. As a precaution, before finishing the planning of your pool, dig several holes in the proposed site to the maximum planned depth to check for roots and other conditions that may get in your way.

A pond without animals and plants can be one depth throughout. However, to include fish and plants, the pool should have a variety of depths. Here's what each requires.

FISH: Although surface area tends to be more important for fish than depth, depth does play a role. The vast majority of fish thrive in standard depths of 18 to 24 inches, but koi (because of their large size) require water at least 3 feet deep. Orfes and goldfish do fine in shallow water as long as the water stays reasonably cool and oxygenated.

Some ponds, especially those in cold areas, need deep zones in which fish can overwinter. In areas where average winter temperatures are from 5° to minus 20° F, the pool should have a section that is 24 inches deep to ensure an unfrozen area for fish. If you live in an area where temperatures drop below that,

A pond with a variety of depths can support many different plants. Here, two shallow-water marginals, blue rabbitsear iris and red 'Fireglow' griffiths spurge, thrive near water lilies, which demand water at least a foot or so deep.

WATER DEPTHS

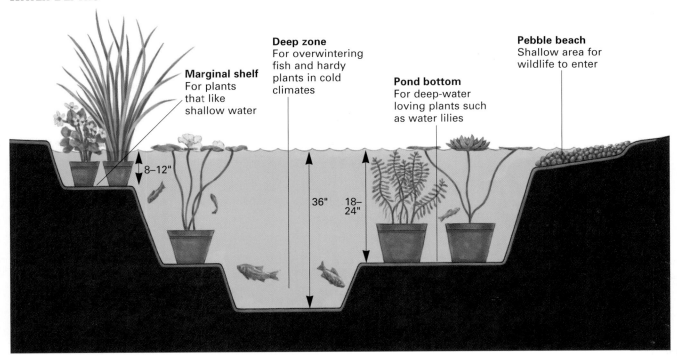

Marginal shelf
For plants that like shallow water

Deep zone
For overwintering fish and hardy plants in cold climates

Pond bottom
For deep-water loving plants such as water lilies

Pebble beach
Shallow area for wildlife to enter

8–12"

36" 18–24"

the deep zone should be 36 inches deep. These deep areas are also excellent spots to overwinter less hardy water plants.

MARGINAL PLANTS: Marginal plants, such as cattails and pickerel rush, are useful design tools in water gardening. With their feet in the water and their heads in the air and sun, they create a smooth transition from the pool to its borders to the landscape.

Most marginals rest on an 8- to 12-inch-deep soil or rigid-liner-shelf. While each plant has different depth requirements, nearly all do well with their crowns either level with the water surface or as much as 2 inches beneath it. When calculating the depth for the marginal shelf, remember to include the pot and plant size. Tall plants, for example, will need fairly wide and deep containers but their crowns still need to be near the water surface.

SUBMERGED PLANTS: Although some of these plants are completely submerged, others will occasionally thrust flower spikes above the water surface. Planted in pots or baskets on the bottom of the pond, most of them should be placed deep enough to reach their mature height without surfacing. The depth for each plant differs. Many require water 3 feet deep; others do fine in just a few inches of water. When deciding the depth of your pond, do a little research on submerged plants to make sure none of your favorites will be too tall for your planned water garden.

WATER LILIES AND OTHER PLANTS WITH FLOATING LEAVES: Many plants for garden pools, including water lilies, grow from roots anchored in pots in the lower parts of

the pond and send up leaves that float on the surface of the water. Plant the smallest of these varieties, such as miniature water lilies, in water as shallow as 6 inches. You can also place them among the plants on the shelf for marginals. Provide the others with water that's 12 to 24 inches deep. Place them on the bottom of the pond. Some floaters have a substantial spread, so if you're planning to grow several, make sure there's room for all.

WILDLIFE: Small amphibians, birds, and many other animals appreciate a gentle surface at the edge of the pond, usually in the form of a pebble beach. Make the beach 4 to 6 inches deep at its deepest point, with a lip at the submerged end to prevent the pebbles from washing into the deeper part of the pond. You can also mortar a row of stones along the edge to prevent them from washing in.

The entire stretch from shore to dropoff, (including the underwater portion) should be at least 2 to 3 feet long with one third of that submerged. Underlay the entire beach surface with flexible liner and use washed sand, pea gravel, pebbles, or all three for the beach itself. (Avoid sharp sand or stone that might damage the liner.)

Keep in mind that pebble beaches have a drawback; they are prone to filamentous algae. If you're not diligent in pulling it out by hand, you'll have to be tolerant of algae growth in late summer.

HINT

Get a plant at just the right depth with the help of stacked red bricks or black plastic storage crates. Do not use concrete in your pond; it can be toxic if it is not properly cured.

ELECTRICAL WORK

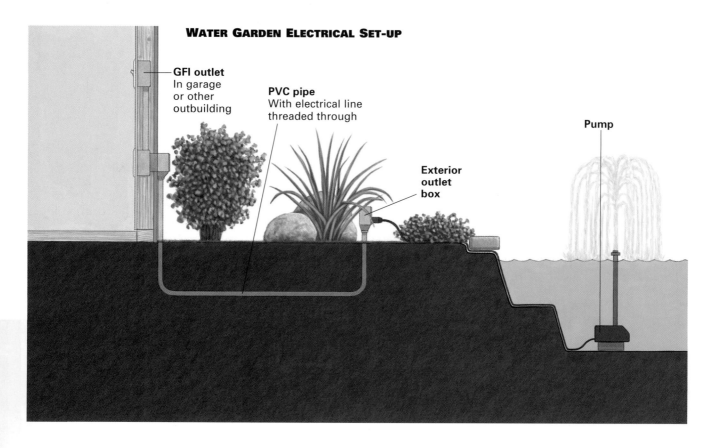

WATER GARDEN ELECTRICAL SET-UP

GFI outlet
In garage
or other
outbuilding

PVC pipe
With electrical line
threaded through

**Exterior
outlet
box**

Pump

Although you can have a delightful garden pool without electricity, power is what creates that splash from a fountain, ensures water clarity with a filter, sparks dazzling effects with lights, and warms the pond with a heater in winter.

While nearly all elements of a modest-size water garden are do-it-yourself projects, the electrical work is one area that most homeowners should leave to professionals. Only those who have extensive experience in electrical work should attempt to wire a water feature themselves. Even then, some codes require that a professional do the work.

CODES

Before you finish planning your water feature, check codes in your area to see whether professional installation is required, how far the water feature must be from the electrical outlet, and whether electrical lines must be buried (and how). And, even if you hire a professional, familiarize yourself with the electrical requirements of your garden pool. You'll do better planning and will be able to discuss the project knowledgeably with the electrician, giving that person all the necessary information.

CIRCUITS

The most important part of a safe water feature is running it on a GFI (sometimes called GFCI), a ground-fault circuit interrupter. You've probably seen them in bathrooms—they're the ones with a red test light or button. These circuits are very sensitive and automatically shut off if they're sliced through or come in contact with moisture (or with you). If a GFI isn't near your water feature, you must have one installed, a cost of about $100 when done by an electrician.

The closer the water feature is to the electrical outlet, the more economical the project will be. Extending lines into the garden costs more, and after 100 feet, voltage begins to drop slightly.

Water garden accessories can be run on three different voltages: 120 volt, 240 volt, and 12 volt. You can use your home's existing

HINT

When designing your water feature, consider installing a separate switch inside the house. You'll be able to turn on fountains and lights with the touch of a finger without going outside.

120-volt AC system to power most pumps, filters, lights, and other pond accessories. The disadvantage of using a 120-volt system is that you may need to bury the cable in protective piping as well as get a permit to do the work.

If your electrical needs will be substantial, consider installing 240-volt service, especially if the pond will have a heavy-duty recirculating pump and fountains (check your pump requirements). This service is able to carry more power, and must be installed by professional electricians.

An alternative lighting power source is a low-voltage system. These 12-volt systems present less danger of shock, so the cable can lay on top of the ground or be buried only an inch or so beneath the soil. Installing them usually doesn't require an electrician or a permit. They extend from a plug-in transformer, which reduces regular household current to 12 volts, and you can install them in about an hour.

OUTLETS: Small pumps and accessories plug into 120-volt outlets. However, it's safest if the outlet is 4 to 6 feet from the water. Some local ordinances require it be that far away.

For large pumps, 15 to 20 amps or greater, you'll need to wire the cord directly into the circuit with the connection enclosed in a weatherproof junction box near the pond, preferably in an inconspicuous spot.

Even if you plan to simply plug the pump into an outlet, an electrician will have to install a weatherproof, outdoor outlet box if the water feature is very far from the house. The outlet is usually mounted a few inches off the ground on a metal post and can be tucked behind a shrub or plant.

WIRING: Protect buried wire by running it through PVC electrical conduit. Bury the conduit at least 18 inches deep.

You can use extension cords (no more than one length at a time) if the pool is close to the electrical source. If you use one, it should be a heavy-duty, three-pronged, grounded, outdoor type of cord. Do not bury connecting ends because they are not waterproof. Instead, keep them above ground and disguise them with rocks or plants in a spot where they will not be disturbed by lawn mowers, power trimmers, or anything else. Wrap electrical tape

Electricity adds a whole new element to a water garden. It powers fountains, pumps, filters, and lights, which can expand your enjoyment of the landscape.

HINT

Carefully read labels on electrical equipment to make sure it has been UL approved.

around the connection to prevent moisture from seeping into the wiring, which will trip the GFI.

Be sure your pond won't overload the circuit. If in doubt, check with an electrician. Otherwise, you may have blown fuses and the expense of extra electrical work after you thought installation was complete.

Estimate the ability of the circuit to carry the additional load by adding up the total wattage of all bulbs and appliances that are plugged into the circuit, including those that are plugged in only occasionally. A 15-amp circuit can handle a continuous load of 1440 watts. A 20-amp circuit can handle 1920 watts.

DIGGING

The most daunting part of creating a large garden pond is the digging. But with some advance planning—and when done properly—digging can be downright fun.

ADVANCE PLANNING

When planning your garden pond, take into consideration how much digging you can do and adjust either the size of the water garden or the amount you do alone. Digging even a small pool is not a job for a person with a history of back pain or heart problems.

GETTING HELP: If you can't dig it yourself, consider hiring a neighborhood teen, or get friends and relatives to help. For very large projects, you may want to hire a backhoe operator. As a rule, water gardens with a surface area of less than 250 square feet are most economically built by hand; larger projects are best done with a backhoe.

DIGGING A POOL

1. Mark the outline of the pond with a garden hose, rope, or sprinkle a line of flour, fine soil, or garden lime. Live with the outline for a week or so to discover how well the new feature fits into the landscape and how it will affect traffic patterns.

2. Remove turf. Use it to fill bare spots in the lawn or set it aside in a pile of its own to compost. If you have a large quantity, use it as the base of a berm or a raised bed. Stack it in the spot for the berm, then cover with several inches of topsoil.

3. As you dig, keep the pond edge level. If it is not level, the liner will show. Check by resting a carpenters level on a straight board laid across the pond. Work all around the pond, checking every shelf and side of the pool so that there are no surprises.

4. Create a spot to overwinter plants and fish. In cold areas, you'll need a zone in the pool that won't freeze. It should be up to 3 feet deep and as wide as it is deep. Be sure this deep zone isn't in the same spot you want to place a pump or fountain.

5. Dig the shelf for the marginal plants about 8 to 12 inches deep. Position the marginal-plant shelf so that the plants frame your view of the water garden. Then dig a ledge for the edging as deep as the edging material and slightly less wide.

6. Toss the soil into a wheelbarrow or onto a tarp to protect your lawn. If it's in good condition, use it to fill in other spots in the landscape, to build a slope for a waterfall, or haul it to a construction site that needs fill dirt.

TIME: Allow plenty of time for digging, considering both pool size and soil type. A small, 18-inch-deep 3-foot by 5-foot pool in sandy soil may take only an hour or so, while a 24-inch-deep, 6-foot by 10-foot pool in clay can take a day or more. Pace yourself. Even if you're in good shape, divide larger projects into one-hour increments with a half-hour rest in between so you don't strain your back.

TOOLS: Make sure your tools are in excellent condition and well-suited to the task. Start with a sharp pointed-blade spade. You'll also need a wheelbarrow for hauling dirt and possibly a truck to haul away soil.

It's best to dig when the soil is moist but not wet. That allows the spade to cut through the soil neatly, and the soil isn't overly heavy. If the weather has been dry, you can moisten the top foot or so of soil by soaking it with water from a hose. Let the soil drain before you start digging.

project, place a carpenters level on a straight piece of 2×4, checking all around the pond.

For a large project, put a stake in the center of the pond with its top at the planned water level. Rest one end of a long straight board on the stake and the other end on the edge of the pool. Check the level. Rotate the board a few feet, again noting the level. Repeat until you return to the starting point.

Use the removed sod to patch bare spots in the yard or add it to a compost pile. If the topsoil is in reasonably good condition, add it to the vegetable garden, spread it on flower beds, or create new beds and berms. If you're installing a rigid liner, set aside the soil to backfill around the liner. Put the soil in a wheelbarrow or on a large tarp or piece of plastic to protect the lawn. Discard clay-laden subsoil or use it to build up a slope for a waterfall. Dump larger amounts at a landfill.

DIGGING IN

Start by marking the site with a garden hose, rope, or garden lime. Then fine-tune the outline with stakes (every foot or so) and twine. Cut along the outline with a spade, then remove the top layer of sod. If you're going to use turf as edging, cut the sod approximately 4 inches in from the outline of the pond. Remove the sod inside the outline and peel back the 4-inch strip. After installing the liner, flip the sod back over it.

To edge with stones or other material, dig an outwardly sloping shelf (6 to 8 inches wide by 2 inches deep) for the liner and the edging. The trench should be deep enough for the edging stones to sit flush with the ground or 3 to 4 inches deep for a concrete footing for edges that will get heavy traffic.

With the sod removed, mark the outlines for marginal shelves, then begin digging from the center outward. Dig 2 inches deeper than the pool depth to allow for sand underlayment (less for other materials). As you dig, angle the sides slightly, about 20 degrees, and make sure the edges of the pond are level or the liner will show. With a small

PROPER DIGGING TECHNIQUE

Digging the wrong way   **Digging the right way**

Digging your garden pond correctly will save you a lot of minor aches and pains as well as possible serious injury.

Wear the proper clothes. A good pair of heavy boots helps you plant your feet, keeps you from slipping, and lets you work more efficiently, reducing fatigue. While digging, be sure to keep a straight back and good posture. Don't stoop or let your shoulders slump. Also, keep your knees bent at all times. This distributes weight to your legs. Lift with your legs, not just with your back.

Work when the soil is reasonably moist—but not wet— to minimize the effort of cutting into the earth without adding much weight to the soil. Scoop up small amounts of soil at a time. Keep loads on the spade reasonably small to prevent strain. Grip the spade close to the blade to give yourself better control.

When tossing soil out of the pond, walk with knees slightly bent to where you'll dump it. Don't stretch out your body to toss the soil in a pile far away; this will overextend your back. As soon as the hole is large enough, step into it and work from the inside.

HINT

Keep good-quality topsoil—which you can reuse—and poorer quality subsoil—which you should discard—separate by tossing them onto two different pieces of plastic or tarp.

INSTALLING FLEXIBLE LINER

Installing flexible liner is fairly simple. Although one person can accomplish the job, it goes faster with two.

Flexible liner has become popular largely because it's easy to install. However, you must install it properly to prevent the liner from showing (which speeds UV deterioration) and leaks from developing.

PREPARATION

LINER: After digging and ensuring that the edges of the pond are level, remove any rough edges—roots, rocks, debris, buried shards of glass—anything that might puncture the lining.

Spread out the liner in the sun for an hour or two to let it soften, which makes it much easier to work with.

If you need to seam two pieces, do it now, using solvent cement or adhesive designed especially for this purpose.

Avoid dragging the liner over the ground or rocks and gravel; this may cause rips or punctures.

HINT

When it's time to install edging, keep flexible liner in place while you work by pushing large nails through the edge of the liner into the soil every foot or so.

UNDERLAYMENT: Underlayment cushions the liner, adding to its life, and preventing rocks and twigs from puncturing it. Use a layer of damp sand, old carpet, or underlayment made specifically for use with flexible liner. The layer should be ½ to 2 inches thick, depending on the material.

Cover the sides as well as the bottom of the pool with the underlayment. Many lining materials are easier to work with if you wet them first, especially when applying them up the sides of the pool. Also, cut triangles in fabric materials to fit the contours.

INSTALLATION

SPREADING: Depending on the size of your garden pond, spreading the liner may take one or several people. Try flapping it like a sheet (up and down) to force air under the liner and help it float into place. As much as possible, smooth out the liner and fold it neatly to fit into the contours and corners of the pond. Don't stretch the liner.

Leave a little wrinkle of extra liner in the bottom of the pond—"pinch an inch" here or there. This allows the liner to spread a little when the soil settles and is particularly wise in earthquake-prone areas. Leave as much excess liner as possible (at least 6 inches) over the outside edge of the pool. Use bricks or stones to hold it in place temporarily.

ADDING WATER: Fill the pool with a few inches of water, then readjust the liner, once again pleating, folding, or arranging it to get as smooth a fit as possible. Move the bricks if needed. Fill the pond about halfway and adjust the liner and bricks again. Folds and wrinkles will always occur. Once adjustments are made, fill the pond almost completely.

EDGING: Trim the liner with heavy scissors or a utility knife, leaving enough excess to protect the edging shelf. Cover the edging liner with soil (or concrete if the edge around the pond must support heavy traffic or a heavy edging material). Then you can install the edging, letting it overhang the pond by at least 2 to 3 inches.

OTHER USES FOR LINER

To repair a cracked concrete pond, drain it, remove any gravel, sand, or other grit, and lay in underlayment—especially important because concrete can abrade holes in the liner. Position the liner, trim it, then lay new edging. To line a wooden whiskey barrel or box, use the same procedure, but staple the liner in place above the water line.

EDGING TIP

Here's a good way to prevent the liner from showing. Dig the edging shelf deep enough for a double layer of flagstones, cut stones, bricks, or other edging. Lay the first layer of edging, then wrap the liner over the first layer as shown and top with the second. Water can now be filled to the middle of the first layer of edging. With one layer of edging, the water can be filled only a little below the bottom of the edging.

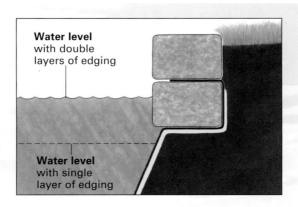

Water level
with double
layers of edging

Water level
with single
layer of edging

INSTALLING LINER, STEP BY STEP

1. CUSHION THE HOLE WITH UNDERLAYMENT. This can be moist sand, old carpet, or underlayment made for water gardens. Cover both the bottom and the sides. Laying underlayment can be frustrating; cut triangles at corners and curves to help fit contours.

2. POSITION LINER. Let the liner warm in the sun for at least an hour to soften. Drape it loosely in the hole, arranging and pleating as needed. (This may be a job for two or more people.) Anchor the sides with bricks or stones, taking care to not stretch the liner.

3. ADJUST THE LINER. Add a few inches of water to the pool to settle the liner. Pleat and tuck the liner, as necessary, to make it fit the contours and corners of the water feature.

4. PREPARE FOR EDGING. Fill the pond with a few more inches of water. Adjust liner, then fill to just below the edging shelf. Trim the liner.

5. INSTALL EDGING. This can be flagstone, brick, cut stone, or other edging. Do a final trim of the liner. You can pat a little soil in behind the edging to conceal any visible liner.

INSTALLING PREFORMED LINER

Although rigid liner is a little more difficult to install than flexible liner, it's still relatively simple. The key is ensuring the liner is level at all times.

Start by putting the liner in position before you begin to dig. You may need to use bricks to hold up portions of the liner if it has varying depths. Level the liner as much as possible. Then pound stakes every foot or so around the liner following the contour of its lip. Further mark around it with rope, a garden hose, flour, or garden lime. Then dig the hole to conform to the shape of the liner, measuring frequently to check depths and widths. The hole needs to be larger than the liner—allow an extra 2 inches around its perimeter and 2 to 3 inches at the bottom. Remove any rocks or sharp objects as you work. Set the liner in place to see if it fits, and make adjustments as needed.

Remove the liner and fill the bottom of the hole with a combination of sand and fine soil. Level this mix with a short board (called a screed), then firmly tamp the soil to create a stable base. Make sure the bottom, marginal shelves, and edges are still absolutely level in all directions after tamping. For large ponds, set the level on a straight piece of lumber.

Again, place the liner in the hole, pressing it down gently so that it fits snugly in the deepest areas. Recheck for level. You may need to remove the liner several times to make adjustments.

Once the pond is perfectly level, fill the bottom with 4 inches of water to stabilize it. Then begin backfilling around the sides of the pond with a mixture of sand and fine soil, checking for level as you go. Tamp the soil-sand mixture in gently with a shovel handle or the end of a 2×4. Be certain to fill all voids and pockets, especially around and under the marginal shelves.

INSTALLING A PREFORMED LINER

1. Position the liner where you plan to locate the pond, using bricks if necessary to keep it level. Then, pound stakes in place around the liner and use them as a guide to mark the exact outline. If the pool is small, make a template by tracing around the lip on cardboard instead.

2. Dig out the shape of the liner, making it 2 inches wider and 2 to 3 inches deeper than the actual liner. Conform your digging to the shape of shelves and deep zones, measuring depth, width, and level frequently. Monitor your work by lowering the liner into place and making adjustments.

3. Once the hole is dug, make sure there aren't any sharp objects or stones left on the bottom. Then fill the bottom with moist sand, fine soil, or a combination of the two. Use a short board to level the bottom. Tamp it down firmly and check the level once again.

Fill the pond with another 4 inches of water. Never allow the water level to be higher than the backfill or the liner may bulge outward. Add more backfill, then 4 more inches of water. Repeat until you have completed the backfilling and the pond is full.

Make preparations for the edging. If the liner has a flat lip, work a foundation of crushed stone topped with damp sand under the lip and around liner edges. Then position the stone or other edging on top of the edge.

If the lip is concave or otherwise can't hold the weight of the edging (or heavy traffic), dig and pour a 3- to 4-inch deep concrete footing that extends beyond and over the top of the lip. Embed the edging in the concrete, overhanging the inside of the liner by 1 to 2 inches. The weight of the edging will be supported by the concrete foundation.

Mortar between the stones, and after it has cured (about a week), scrub with muriatic acid to neutralize the lime. Drain the pond (runoff from the acid will make the water toxic), rinse, and refill.

HINT

If you need to clean the liner, spray with water from a garden hose. Never scrub a liner; it can easily be damaged.

4. Lower the liner into place, checking the level. You may need to remove the liner several times to make adjustments.

5. Add 4 inches of water and begin backfilling. Tamp the soil with a shovel handle or 2×4 as you work. Backfill again and add 4 more inches of water, keeping the water level no higher than the backfill. Repeat until filled.

PREFORMED LINERS ABOVE GROUND

Working with a rigid liner is even easier and faster when building an aboveground pool.

It's ideal—but not absolutely necessary—to partially bury the liner so that its marginal shelves are flush with the soil surface. (Partly burying it helps stabilize water temperatures.) Dig the hole 2 inches wider on the sides and 2 inches deeper on the bottom. Add sand, tamp it down, then position the liner, making sure it's exactly level. Fill the unit with 4 inches of water to stabilize it. Backfill to ground level, tamping with a 2×4 or the back of your spade.

Then add the siding. Siding can be a wood frame, stacked flagstones, cut stone, concrete pavers, wooden flower border edging, logs set on end, or other materials. As you install the siding, backfill along the sides of the rigid liner with soil and moist sand to support the sides of the liner. Depending on the type of siding, you may want to leave pockets of soil between the liner and the siding in which to insert plants to soften the liner edges.

If setting the pond into the side of a hill, be sure to set it out 6 inches to 1 foot from the slope to prevent erosion. It's an especially good idea to partly bury the bottom of the liner that's placed on a hill to prevent the pond from sliding out of place. Backfill around the bottom and behind the side of the pond that faces the hill.

MAKING A STONE-SIDED POOL

1. Rigid liner works well for creating aboveground ponds with stone sides. Flexible liner can tear in such installations. Choose a fiberglass pool with a flat lip, which will best withstand weather extremes and support the weight of stone edging. For the easiest, least expensive, and lowest maintenance pond, dig a hole and sink the liner to the depth of its marginal shelves. By burying part of the liner, you minimize masonry work and stabilize pool temperatures in summer.

2. Set in each course of stone slightly toward the liner. Backfill behind each course as you go. Lay the first course far enough away from the liner to allow for sufficient inset. (Experiment before you start—lay a trial side until the height and inset is correct.)

3. Carefully backfill under the lip of the liner with a mixture of moist sand and fine soil. For additional strength, pack concrete under the lip. Conceal the liner edge by slightly overhanging the edging to the inside of the pond. Position the edging so as little weight as possible rests on the liner lip.

When skillfully designed and surrounded by stone, an aboveground pool blends beautifully into the landscape.

INSTALLING ABOVEGROUND POOLS

Even if you don't have hard-to-dig, problem soil, an aboveground pool may suit you. Not only are aboveground pools and ponds good options where digging would be difficult, but they're also appealing in their ability to raise the water up close, which is especially nice near a patio or other sitting area.

Raised and semiraised water features tend to take longer than sunken ponds to build and usually cost more. However, they're less likely to become cluttered with blowing debris or eroding soil.

TYPES OF POOLS: Aboveground pools are as varied as the gardeners who install them. The only requirement is that they be built from materials sturdy enough to withstand the outward pressure of water. Aboveground water features are often made of brick, an excellent material in formal gardens or in landscapes that already contain a lot of brick. Concrete block—veneered with stucco, brick, tile, or stone—is another option. Wood timbers stacked upon each other, lumber fashioned into a charming box, or logs stacked on end in a row provide other possibilities. Raised water features can also be made of cut or natural stone.

HEIGHT: The height of an aboveground pool can vary from just 1 foot to much higher. For a pool that's completely above ground, the ideal height is between 24 and 30 inches, especially if you want passersby to see the fish or to be able to sit on the edge.

The pool should be a minimum of 18 inches deep. For a pool that rises above ground less than that height, partially excavate the pool to make it 18 inches deep. By doing this, the feature will also be better insulated from the elements.

FOOTINGS: A masonry aboveground pool will need a concrete footing around the perimeter of its base. The depth of the footing depends on your climate, but it may need to be as deep as 2 feet in northern regions. Check local codes for proper depth. You can pour the footing directly into a trench; in soft soil you may need to build wooden forms with 2×4s for the footing. Either way, make sure the footing is perfectly level from one side to the other.

MATERIALS: Wooden raised pools are simple to make; masonry projects require more time and skill. Structures made of wood are most successful when constructed from pressure-treated lumber or redwood to prevent rot. The wood should be relatively smooth to prevent flexible liner from ripping during installation.

No matter what material you use for the sides of your raised feature, the pool will need to be underlayed and lined. Rigid liner works well for raised gardens, but flexible liner offers more options for style and shape, limited only by your imagination. Staple the liner to the edges of wooden structures or glue it to them with silicone sealant. In masonry projects, sandwich the liner between the last course of brick and the cap.

Just like their sunken counterparts, above-ground pools support a variety of plants and fish. Potted plants at its base help this pool further blend into its surroundings.

MAKING A WOOD-SIDED POOL

1. Build wood-sided pools with rot-resistant wood and rust-resistant hardware. Measure and cut all materials before assembly. The pool shown here will use flexible liner. If using a rigid liner, allow room for backfill. Predrill at the corners and at 8- to 10-inch intervals along the wall for corner and side ties. Use all-thread—long steel rod threaded along its length—or concrete rebar for the ties. Bury the first course in the soil slightly, by half its height, to improve stability.

2. If the pool is large or will sit completely above ground, add a 2-inch layer of sand on the bottom. (Use plywood for the bottom of small pools on a deck or patio.) Insulate and protect the pool by covering interior sides of the box with old carpet, water garden underlayment, or smooth plywood. As you construct the pool, check frequently to make certain all sides are level.

3. Position the liner, pleating carefully. Fill the bottom 4 inches, do a final check on level, and reposition the liner if necessary. (Even a very small pool weighs hundreds of pounds when filled so reposition now.) Then fill the pool halfway. Staple the liner in place above the final water level, being careful that no stretching of the liner will take place once it's filled. Create a cap along the top to give the pool a finished look and conceal the liner edge.

BOG GARDENS

Abog garden is a wonderful solution to several landscaping challenges. A freestanding bog garden creates the perfect microclimate for moisture-loving plants. A bog garden attached to a pool or pond makes the pond look more natural, providing a transition to the rest of the landscape and attracting wildlife. A bog garden is also a solution for a low or chronically wet spot where plants that prefer drier soil do not thrive.

Bog gardens are among the easiest water features to install and maintain. Simply put, they are beds of moisture-retentive soil spread over a pond liner, which helps the soil retain water.

Most plants that do well as marginals in a pond also do well as bog plants. Gardeners in moist climates can create bog gardens for plants with high moisture requirements—such as water iris, cattail, umbrella palm, and aquatic grasses. Gardeners in dry climates, especially those in the West, can use a bog garden to grow plants with more modest water requirements that would otherwise not do well in their region.

USABLE LOCATIONS

If you have a low spot that naturally collects water, it may be the perfect site for a bog garden. An area where the soil is heavy clay with slow drainage, or a low-lying area that collects rain are good possibilities. Even a location near a downspout or other clean water drainage could serve as a bog garden. Also consider creating a mini bog garden in a container; simply plug any holes and plant accordingly. Because most plants for bog gardens are sun lovers, locate the garden on a site that receives six or more hours of direct light a day.

A bog garden's marsh-like conditions allow you to grow an array of wonderful plants that otherwise wouldn't thrive in a home garden.

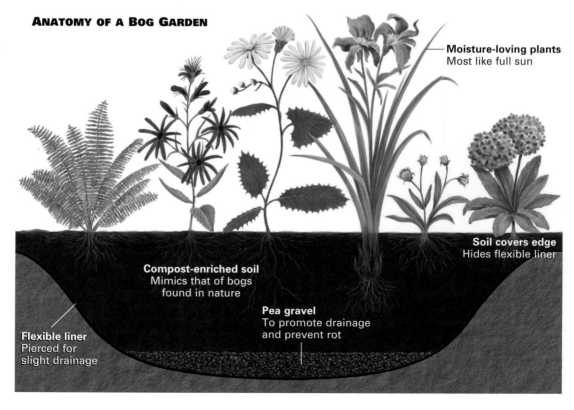

ANATOMY OF A BOG GARDEN

Moisture-loving plants
Most like full sun

Soil covers edge
Hides flexible liner

Compost-enriched soil
Mimics that of bogs found in nature

Pea gravel
To promote drainage and prevent rot

Flexible liner
Pierced for slight drainage

FREESTANDING OR CONNECTED?

You can create the bog so its water supply is completely independent of the pond, or erect a small, water-permeable dam to allow water to percolate into the bog.

A bog independent of a pond has an advantage over a connected bog—it's easier to maintain the ideal moisture level in the bog. Just water when the soil seems too dry. Also, you can fertilize an independent bog with less danger that chemicals will seep into the pond.

To create an independent bog, build an earthen dam between it and the pond, making sure the dam comes up to or above the water level. Cover the dam with flexible liner, disguise it with stone, and water the bog independently.

To interconnnect the pond with the bog, continue the flexible liner from the pool into the bog (at a depth of 6 to 18 inches). Construct a stone dam between the bog and the pond, on top of the liner. Leave a hole or two in the dam so water can seep in, or insert a couple of lengths of PVC pipe through the dam. You can line the inside face of the rock dam with plastic liner so soil from the bog doesn't wash into the pond, leaving the holes or pipe uncovered.

SPECIFIC NEEDS OF BOGS

LINER AND DRAINAGE: The bottom layer of a bog should consist of an inch or two of pea gravel. The gravel allows water to drain away from the soil when the soil is saturated.

Because the liner isn't exposed to sun—its edges are buried just under the soil surface—you can use inexpensive polyethylene sheeting rather than a heavier duty liner.

Bog plants need moisture, but they also need some drainage. When installing the bog in heavy clay soil, pierce the liner about every 3 feet with a garden fork (less in well-drained soils). If you find out later that drainage is too slow, you can increase it by pounding a long

The brilliant yellow flag iris is one of the most popular plants for bogs and waterside plantings.

This bog garden is resplendent in late spring with irises and primulas.

EASIEST BOG PLANTS

Aquatic grasses	Pickerel rush
Cardinal flower	Arrowhead
Cattail	Umbrella palm
Creeping jenny	Water iris
Horsetail	Water canna
Marsh marigold	

HINT

If you're concerned about soil eroding into a pond, cover the surface of the bog soil with an inch or so of sand or gravel.

BOG GARDENS
continued

stake into the soil and through the liner. Exercise care when increasing the drainage of a bog that gets its water from a pool or stream. If the bog drains too much, the rest of the feature will also lose water.

In dry climates, consider an irrigation system for your bog. The simplest system is a length of soaker hose or perforated pipe along the bottom of the bog. Run the soaker hose or pipe to the soil surface and connect it to a garden hose to allow water to seep slowly and evenly into the soil.

SOIL: Soil in a bog garden must be exceptionally high in humus. Good quality topsoil should be mixed half and half with fine or sifted compost. This mimics the soil found in marshes and other wetlands, where plant matter quickly breaks down, continually replenishing the soil. Sphagnum peat moss from natural bogs also is a good addition, holding many times its weight in water. It might, however, inhibit the growth of some plants, so use it sparingly until you get to know the plants.

PLANTS: A wide variety of plants that thrive in shallow water also do well in bogs. Many marginals, such as yellow flag and cardinal flower, do especially well in bogs. However, be ready to experiment to see what plants do best in your particular bog. Soil, moisture, and regional climate can vary radically from bog garden to bog garden. If one plant doesn't work, try another. If the soil mix is too rich and rots the roots, work in a high-quality topsoil or vermiculite to lighten it.

It's important to keep your bog constantly moist, which can be a challenge during late summer. Because some of the plants will grow in standing water but others won't, test for soil dryness to a depth of at least 4 or 5 inches. If the soil is not almost soggy, water deeply.

Fertilize your bog garden periodically with compost. Avoid using slow-release fertilizers. They break down too quickly in wet conditions.

These irises, natural wetland inhabitants in the wild, find conditions to their liking in the rich, wet soil of a backyard bog garden.

HINT

If you install an irrigation system in your bog, attach a quick-release hose coupler to the end of the system and the end of your hose for ease of use.

MAKING A BOG

1. Dig a hole 6–18 inches deep in an area receiving at least six hours of sun a day. A low-lying or poorly drained area is perfect. So is a site next to a pool or pond, where it's easy to keep the bog's soil moist.

2. Line the pond. Spread inexpensive liner over the hole. Pierce it every 3 feet or so with a garden fork. Spread 1–2 inches of pea gravel on the bottom of the hole. Trim the liner so it will be concealed under the soil surface.

3. To create a dam, either build one of earth while you're digging or make one of rocks positioned between the bog and pond. Place liner against the rocks to prevent soil from washing into the pond. Leave holes in the dam or insert PVC pipe to create a passage for water.

4. Fill the bog with high-quality, moisture-retentive topsoil. You can also mix in sphagnum peat moss, but use it sparingly at first to see how plants react to it. Plant moisture-loving species in the bog and water them well. Fertilize occasionally with compost.

FOUNTAINS: PLANNING

A fountain packs a lot of charm into a small space. Whether traditional or contemporary, it propels a stream of water through the air and creates a cooling effect. It's ideal for up-close viewing, which is why fountains are usually located on a porch, patio, or other sitting area.

A fountain can attach to a wall or stand alone. Some freestanding fountains are designed to rest in—or next to—a pool or pond, while others are water features unto themselves, working well on a deck, patio, lawn, or tucked into a flower bed. Tabletop fountains have recently become popular, taking just minutes to set up.

Fountains fit into any style garden. This one, which is designed from an old-fashioned hand pump, would work well in a casual setting.

You can choose from a wide variety of styles, colors, materials, and sizes. However, choose a fountain that is in keeping with the overall style of your garden and home. A classical statuary fountain might look out of place in a simple country garden, for example. A wall fountain fashioned of brick and stone or stone look-alike is best set against similarly sturdy masonry—not wood—siding.

Most fountains are made of precast concrete. Reconstituted stone and fiberglass have also become popular, simulating the look of stone with amazing realism. Whether concrete or stone look-alike, fountains come in numerous colors and surface finishes. Finding just the right fountain for your garden takes some research. Visit garden centers to scout their offerings. Ask if there are other fountains that you can special order. Also check out mail-order catalogs. If you want a special, one-of-a-kind fountain, visit art fairs or ask at art galleries for the names of local artists who might design a fountain for you.

WALL FOUNTAINS

Taking up no floor room, wall fountains are ideal for gardens or seating areas tight on space. Most are powered by a submersible pump that recirculates water from the basin through a delivery pipe up to the spout. Designs are nearly infinite, but most have a jet of water spilling into a trough or basin.

Plumbing some wall fountains can be rather complicated, often requiring piping behind the wall. In other cases, the water lines run on the wall surface and must be

Some fountains are created with a special water-spouting plaque installed on the wall.

disguised with vines or other plants. However, simple-to-install, preformed kits are now available with only a cord running from them. Because the ease and cost of installation varies widely, consider the installation when buying a wall fountain.

Wall fountains attach in several ways. Stone fountains attach with mortar and are supported with special T-blocks, decorative braces that act as brackets. Lighter weight fountain kits come with mounting hardware.

FREESTANDING FOUNTAINS

Appealing because of its ease of installation, a freestanding fountain also makes an ideal focal point for a patio, flower bed, or lawn. In this type of fountain, a small submersible pump is housed in the lower pedestal, in a hollow base beneath the bowl. Its design should allow easy access to the pump so you can clean and maintain it, usually monthly.

STATUARY FOUNTAINS

These ornamental fountains can be placed near a pond or pool or in the water feature itself. The decorative statue has a supply pipe projecting from its base. The pipe is connected to the pump with flexible tubing.

Large statues must have firm footing. For a fountain on the side of a pond, make sure its resting place (including any edging) is firm and level. If you want to install the fountain in the pond, you can mount it on a hollow in-pond pedestal created specifically for that purpose or build your own with mortared bricks or stone. If the statue is small, black plastic storage crates make an easy, hard-to-detect base as long as the base of the fountain is slightly under water.

FOUNTAIN CARE

Fountains in sunny spots tend to have problems with algae. If you are not raising fish or plants in your fountain, you can prevent algae by adding chlorine bleach to the fountain water. Add it at the rate of 2 ounces of bleach to every 10 gallons of water, once a month. If that doesn't work, increase the amount of bleach to 5 ounces. If you do have plants or fish, consider using an algaecide. Make sure it's labeled for use in ponds with fish and plants; follow package directions exactly.

HINT

If you want fish, avoid fountains made of lead. Lead is toxic to fish.

A statuary fountain adds not only splash and movement but also a decorative element that helps set the mood of the water feature.

WEATHERPROOFING YOUR FOUNTAIN

Take good care of your fountain year-round to greatly prolong its life.

One of the best things you can do for concrete fountains and statuary is to apply a concrete sealer to prevent moisture from getting into the concrete and expanding and cracking it when the water freezes. It's also important to drain the fountain before freezing weather arrives to prevent ice from forming on the pump. Ice can crack pump housings and cause seals to fail. It also can crack basins.

If you can, drain the fountain by tipping over the basin. If you can't tip the basin, siphon or pump it out.

Prevent rain, ice, and snow from collecting again in the basin by covering the fountain or statuary with a sheet of plastic. Tie the plastic down well to prevent it from flapping in the wind, which quickly destroys the plastic.

Many pumps will dry out, shrinking the seals and preventing the fountain from working properly. Overwinter your pump in a bucket of water in a basement or heated garage. It's also important that the cord does not dry out; cracked cords can cause dangerous shorts.

FOUNTAINS: INSTALLING

Depending upon the design of your fountain, installation can take just minutes—or a day or more, even with professional help. Here are the basics.

WALL FOUNTAINS

Your wall must be sturdy enough to hold the fountain, its basin, and the water it contains. Most wood-sided walls are not strong enough, but many stucco and brick walls are. Check with a contractor or mason if you're unsure of the wall's stability. You may need to include a decorative T-block fitted to the wall as a bracket to support the basin.

If the plumbing is to be installed through the wall, you'll need to drill holes with a power drill (and masonry bit for stone walls). Drill one hole up high (usually just below eye level) for the water outlet and one low for the water intake. Insert pipe through each hole and join them behind the wall with two elbow joints and a length of flexible pipe.

If the pipe cannot be installed through a wall, you will need to attach it to the surface of the wall. You can chisel a channel into a solid concrete surface to set the pipe flush, but if chiseling will affect the strength of the material (brick or concrete block, for example), use rigid pipe attached to the wall with clamps. Either way, the exterior plumbing must ultimately be disguised with vines or other plants.

Attach the fountain to the wall, usually with a combination of mortar and wall plugs. Connect the pump—if it's not built in—to the intake pipe and plug it into a GFI outlet.

FREESTANDING FOUNTAINS

Most of these come preplumbed and installation is simple. Check the level of the site on which the fountain will rest and make necessary adjustments to even it up.

Position the fountain and again check its level. If you need to adjust the level, use sand, soil, or bits of stone. Fill the fountain and plug it in (to a GFI outlet only). If the cord doesn't reach the outlet, you can use one length of extension cord designed specifically for outdoor use. You can bury the cord just under the soil surface, but do not bury the connection. Instead, leave it above ground, wrap it with waterproof tape, and disguise it with stone, or by setting it among pots or plants.

STATUARY FOUNTAINS

Most statuary fountains are designed for either in-pond or out-of-pond installation, but some can be used in both locations. Where you position your statuary fountain, therefore, depends primarily on its design.

OUT-OF-POND FOUNTAINS: Small out-of-pond statuary fountains can rest on stones on the edge of the pool or stream. Larger out-of-pond fountains need a more substantial base, such as a perfectly level stone or concrete pad. With both, a pump rests in the pond, recirculating water through a flexible tube. You'll need to disguise the tubing and the electrical cord with stone, plants, or soil.

WALL FOUNTAIN

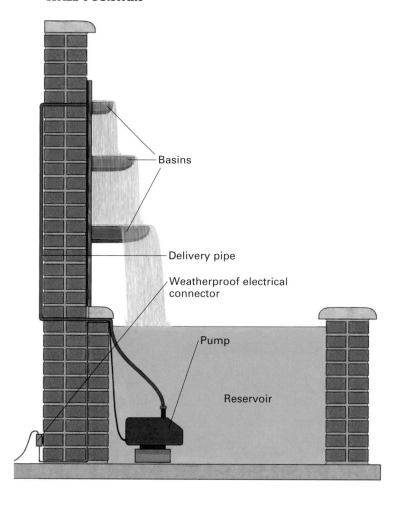

Basins

Delivery pipe

Weatherproof electrical connector

Pump

Reservoir

POSITIONING OUT-OF-POOL STATUARY FOUNTAINS

Out-of-pond fountains are not only an excellent, easy way to add the sound of splashing water to your water garden, they tie it in with the rest of the landscape. And because they're decorative, they add an element of garden art.

Test the position of your out-of-pond fountain by first hooking up the pump and plugging in the fountain. The spray will vary with the design of the fountain but can be made larger or smaller by turning the flow adjuster on the pump. Experiment with placement of the fountain and the power of the flow until you get a pleasing effect. Most out-of-pond fountains look best when set asymmetrically to one side of the water feature.

IN-POND FOUNTAINS: In-pond statuary fountains are usually larger than out-of-pond models. For that reason, they need a solid foundation on which to rest.

Set small fountains weighing under 30 pounds on a stack of bricks. For larger fountains, either build a substantial base from mortared brick or stone, or install a precast concrete pedestal for the foundation. If you're building your own base, be sure to allow a core for any piping that will be connected to the pump (most larger fountains are run by an external pump).

Very large statuary—those over 100 pounds—require footings. Pour at least 6 inches of reinforced concrete in the ground underneath the fountain before installing the underlayment and the liner. Then build or install the pedestal on this footing.

HINT

Before you install your in-pond pedestal, put an extra layer of liner under the pedestal base to prevent tears and leaks.

FREESTANDING FOUNTAIN

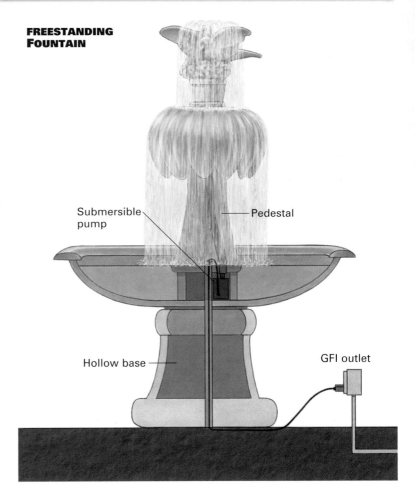

Submersible pump

Pedestal

Hollow base

GFI outlet

STREAMS AND WATERFALLS

You can build streams and waterfalls with the help of modern-day liner and high-quality pumps. A stream can be just a few feet in length or traverse hundreds of feet. It can include ponds and waterfalls in its course or none at all. A waterfall can be as small as a trickle of water tumbling a few inches over the lip of a stone or as dramatic as a cascade dropping several feet. And although waterfalls often appear naturalistic, many beautiful formal gardens incorporate them, too.

PLANNING A STREAM

Before designing your stream, study natural creeks and brooks. Take a walk in one of your state parks or spend some time looking at pictures of water gardens that include streams. Watch how a stream cuts its course, how the banks are formed, where rocks lie, and how plants grow. Note, too, how falls and pools occur. Then take your cue from nature. Naturalizing a stream is the key to making it look like it came with the landscape.

Plan your stream on paper first. Make rough and then refined sketches of your design, but only after you've studied the contours of your landscape.

You can locate a stream just about anywhere in your yard. If your yard has a slope, it will be easy to turn it into a watercourse. However, even if your yard is flat, you can build a slope with infill soil or soil left after digging a pond. You will need only a slight incline (1 to 2 inches for every 10 feet) to keep the water flowing.

The length of the stream will be your first consideration, and of course, no rules apply here, except those that govern your landscape and the limitations of your budget. If, however, your plans include a pond, the total stream length should be twice the length of any ponds so the features are in scale with each other.

Next, decide on the width for the stream. In general, the wider the stream bed, the more leisurely its current; the narrower, the faster the current. The speed of the current, however, can also be determined by the size of your pump. You can have a rapidly flowing stream in a wide bed, for example, if your plans—and budget—allow for a large pump.

The stream will look more natural if you plan to include a series of short, almost-level sections in the streambed. These sections should be level enough to hold some water even when the pump is off. Connect the sections by drop-offs of just an inch or so.

Add whatever twists and turns you can to the stream. Meandering streams look natural. So do streams with rocks and boulders; add them to your plans, too, in a variety of sizes and shapes. Large rocks inside the water course create rivulets by diverting water around them. Smaller rocks and pebbles produce ripples as the water moves over them.

Mini bogs along the stream will also give the impression that the stream was formed by nature, and you should include them in your sketches. These mini bogs are shallow areas—unconnected to the stream—for moisture-loving plants that you dig (and line) a few feet out from the stream. They look (and work) best with rocked and mortared edges and should be filled with water that is independent of the stream. (Don't tap water from the stream; that interferes with its water flow.)

You might want your plans to include the installation of a permanent irrigation system to keep the bogs wet. A soaker hose at the bottom of the mini bog will work, but you can water them by hand, as well. Just make sure you water often enough.

Once your sketch is complete, take your design outside. Mark out the watercourse with a hose or rope. Or, if your design will include one or more waterfalls, read the following section and consider the information as you work to complete your plan.

With the addition of a waterfall, you can turn an ordinary corner of the yard into a spot of extraordinary beauty.

PLANNING A WATERFALL

There is no rule on how many waterfalls you should have. A watercourse can have no falls or can be nothing but falls. The height and width of the falls are also up to you.

However, there is one rule you should follow when planning waterfalls: Keep them in scale with the ponds (called catch basins) they empty into. A small trickle will be lost emptying into a large pond, and will have little value in circulating and oxygenating the water. On the other hand, a waterfall gushing into a small catch basin will disrupt the surface and stir up sediment, creating poor conditions for fish and plants.

At the other end of the waterfall are header pools, a 10-inch (or deeper) pool at the top of every waterfall. Header pools create a more natural look than water simply spilling from an outlet pipe. Include them in your sketches, and remember that if you'd like a series of waterfalls, the catch basin of one is the header pool for the next.

While you're planning, think about what type of falls you want: a smooth, broad, unbroken curtain of water, or a narrow, frothy cascade. The surface of the spill stone (the stone that forms the lip of the fall) determines the way the water falls. For a curtain of water, use a smooth, flat stone. For a frothy cascade, find a spill stone with ridges and bumps, one that funnels water somewhat to its center. Note these on your plans. You may want a different effect in each of a series of waterfalls.

When all your plans are completed, mark out the watercourse and waterfall with rope or a hose. Leave it for a day or two before you dig to see if you like what you've designed.

Then mark the course in further detail with marker stakes on both sides, every foot or so. If you're building up the surface with a berm, put the stakes at the outside edges of the planned berm location with their tops at the height of the soil you will add. Tie a piece of string between them so you can see the height and contour of your water course and waterfalls. Once you've brought in soil, tamp it or let it settle—three months is best. Now you're ready for the digging.

HINT

When planning your waterfall or stream, go through nature, environmental, and outdoor living magazines. Collect photos of streams and waterfalls for ideas to incorporate into your own landscape.

The best-planned streams mimic nature. This stream not only meanders lazily, it also incorporates a variety of stones, scattered throughout in a seemingly random pattern.

This small waterfall helps aerate the water for fish. However, it doesn't disturb the surface so much that water lilies—which love still water—can't thrive.

STREAMS AND WATERFALLS
continued

HINT

Dig stream and catch basins a little larger than you think you want them to be. Once you install edging and stones, they'll look smaller.

EXCAVATION

The first step in building a stream or waterfall is excavation. If you have an existing slope or hill, its overall incline will largely determine the pitch of your water feature. But if you're creating a watercourse on relatively flat land or you want waterfalls with substantial heights, you'll need to build a berm with infill soil. The illustrations on this page and on pages 66 and 67 show the details found in streams and waterfalls.

On either a natural incline or a prepared berm, start by refining the layout of the stream and/or waterfall on your lawn. Move the stakes and twine along the stream sides as you define exactly where your stream will twist and turn. Once you've finalized the course, tie twine from stake to stake at ground level, for areas you'll excavate, and above ground level at the height of the areas to be built up. Also, tie a level line—it attaches to the twine with built-in hooks—across the bed at these locations. Your stakeout and twining now will tell you exactly where to dig and where (and how much) soil should be added.

Dig the pond(s), and any catch basin(s), and header pool(s) first (see pages 44 to 45). Move the excavated soil to locations that need infill, or set it aside on tarps for disposal.

Leave a strip—6 inches to 1 foot wide—around each pool for rocks and edging. If the header pool is large or if you'll be using very large stones, this edge should actually be a ledge—a foot or more wide and roughly half as deep as the diameter of the boulders—cut around the outside of the pools. If you want bogs or damp planting areas along the watercourse, dig them out as well, and make an edge for their borders, too.

Now you're ready for the stream itself. Remember that a stream bed needs a drop of at least 1 to 2 inches every 10 feet to ensure a downhill flow, but beyond that, it can be as steep or as gentle as you want.

Excavate the existing ground (or berm if you've brought in infill) to the depth you've chosen for the entire watercourse, using the level to chart the slope of the bed. On a natural slope, dig generally to the same depth throughout, checking the incline of the bed frequently. In areas within the stream that will be planted, leave level terraces to ensure that plants and other stream life will stay healthy even if the pump breaks down.

Finally, dig out a channel (about 6 inches deep) in which to lay the piping that will return the water from the pond or foot of the stream to its head. Leave a length of tubing exposed at each end for the inlet and outlet. Trench another channel for electric line conduit.

UNDERLAYMENT AND LINER

Once the watercourse is excavated, cover it with underlayment to shield the liner against punctures from roots, stones, or sharp debris. Spread a ½-inch layer of sand, old carpet, or underlayment that's made specifically for

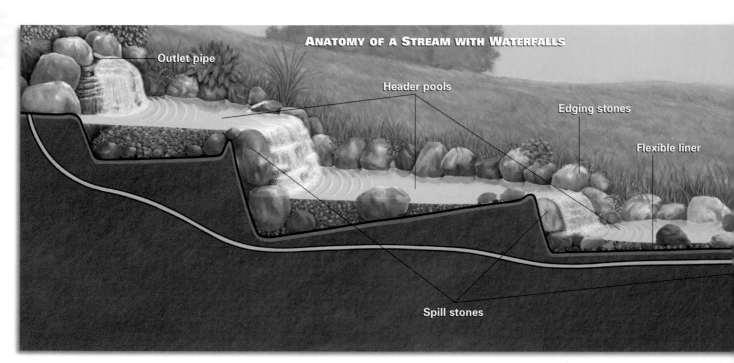

ANATOMY OF A STREAM WITH WATERFALLS

Outlet pipe

Header pools

Edging stones

Flexible liner

Spill stones

water gardens. (You can skip this, of course, if your liner has underlayment attached.)

Following the directions on page 46, fit the liner to the entire excavation. If a single piece of liner can cover the excavated area, merely make adjustments as when laying liner in a pool. Most likely the stream will require more than one section of liner. If so, overlap the sections. Here's how: Start at the bottom of the watercourse. Allow for liner to extend from one section into the next (up and over the lip of a waterfall, for example). Lap each upper section over the lower piece. Seal the seams with adhesive or tape made for this purpose. Sealing allows water to flow over the seam and prevents seepage.

INSTALL THE PUMP: TRIAL RUN

After laying all the liner, place the pump in the lowest part of the stream or pond, setting it on bricks so it won't take in silt. It should be opposite a waterfall, if you have built one. At this location, the pump provides maximum circulation and aeration. Attach the pump to the supply and outlet lines. Now you're ready for a trial run.

Turn on the pump to move water through the course. Let header pools, terraces, and catch basins fill, and as they fill, settle the liner into place. Fill the pool halfway, readjust the liner, then let it fill completely. Make sure that no liner will show after the edging is installed, adding or removing soil beneath the liner to bring the edge level with the water. Trim the liner if you want, but leave enough to go under edging; you'll make the final trim after the stones are set in place.

SOUND

You can control the sound of your watercourse by the way you create waterfalls and strategically position stones.

Part of what affects sound is the water's speed and volume. Large amounts of water moving rapidly produce a gushing sound. A small rivulet moving slowly sounds more like a ripple. Although pleasant if adjusted properly, a ripple that's too weak can sound like a leaky faucet. Fine-tune the sound of your watercourse by turning the flow valve on the pump.

The more falls you design into the watercourse, the louder the sound. And different types of falls create different sounds. A flat fall where water sheets over the edge makes a subtle—even peaceful—sound. A fall where water cascades down the rocks makes quite a splash. Positioning stones behind the falls creates a hollow space that amplifies and echoes sound.

Placing large stones in the stream not only makes the stream look more natural, it also increases the splashing sound. Add, move, or remove large stones until the stream or waterfall sounds just the way you want it.

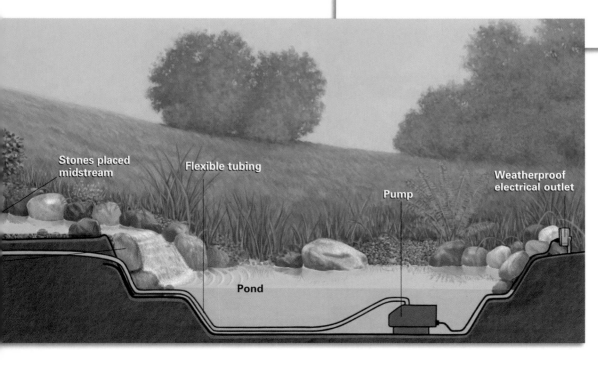

Stones placed midstream

Flexible tubing

Pump

Weatherproof electrical outlet

Pond

STREAMS AND WATERFALLS
continued

EDGING AND POSITIONING STONE

Once the watercourse is lined and the water flow tested, it's time to install the edging. Edging holds the liner in place as well as disguises it. It also helps create a transition from the stream to the surrounding area and makes the watercourse look like it's always been there.

Edging stones can be flat or round and laid in one to three courses or—depending on the contours of the landscape—at random: one course at one location, three at another.

You can set edging stones loosely or mortar them in place. Mortaring isn't required, but it prevents water from flowing under the edging, which increases the water feature's volume without requiring a bigger pump.

Start by placing edging stones along the inside and outside edge of the entire watercourse, including the stream bed, ponds, and mini bogs. You'll probably need to position each rock at least a couple of times to get just the right effect.

Next, build the spillways for waterfalls, if the water feature has them. Lay flat rocks or other materials to form each lip (where water spills over). Their top surface should be slightly below the water level of the stream or

STREAM AND WATERFALL MATERIALS

GRAVEL AND PEBBLES
Use these as a bottom layer, in conjunction with sand, to cover the liner and to create a gravel bed like those found in nature. Pea gravel is widely available, but check out gravel and pebbles from local quarries. As a rule, darker gravel or pebbles create a more striking look. Avoid brightly-colored or white gravel, which looks artificial.

Generally, the larger the rock the less prone it is to collecting algae and silt. Gravel is very prone to algae growth; an assortment of larger stones in the floor of the stream is less likely to create a problem.

ROCKS AND STONE
Excellent for edging material, medium-size rocks and stones can hold down the liner, accent the stream as well as edge it, create a waterfall, and serve many other functions. Choose rocks and stones that look as though they might occur together in nature. Avoid wide contrasts in color such as black lava rock next to limestone. Flat flagstone is invaluable for edging. The more worn and weathered the stone, the more natural it looks.

BOULDERS
Unless you live in a very rocky part of the country, the size of boulders and their expense will mean they can be used only as accents. However, boulders add drama, especially at lower or upper sections of a stream or in a strategic spot that highlights a particularly pretty part of a watercourse. For a natural appearance, partially bury boulders so no more than one- to two-thirds of their surface is visible. If they're in the water, no more than half of their height should be above water.

Set very large boulders on a concrete footing. Cover the footing with underlayment, then with liner. Then place the boulder on the footing. Otherwise, the boulders may settle lower than you want.

header pool that precedes it. That way, water will flow from the header pool to the catch basin without overflowing the banks.

If the lip will be more than a foot or so across, set a foundation stone vertically under the lip stone. You can also lay stones in the header pool just before the lip (in addition to those you've put in place for edging to form channels to direct water to the falls.

Periodically turn on the pump, or use a hose to test the flow and effect of the water, making sure it moves over the falls the way you want. Change lip stones until you get the right effect.

Once the edging and spillways are in place, trim off excess liner, and if you're not mortaring, pat good-quality soil in nooks among the stones to make pockets for plants.

Mortared edging and spillways are more difficult. After you experiment with the stones to get the right arrangement, mortar them in sections. Take out the stones, lay the mortar bed, then replace the stones. Fill in between stones with mortar. Avoid using so much it detracts from the natural look.

Use bagged mortar mix, or mix your own with 1 part lime, 2 parts portland cement, and 9 parts sharp sand. To help the mortar blend in, add a mortar dye that matches the general color of the stone. After the mortar dries, treat it with muriatic acid to cure it and keep it from leaching lime. Lime increases the water pH, which is potentially toxic to fish. Follow label directions and wear protective gear—muriatic acid is extremely dangerous.

After treating the mortar, rinse all concrete surfaces thoroughly to remove acid residue. Do not allow the rinse water to remain in any part of the water feature.

HINT

If you notice an unusual drop in the pond level, you may have a leak. Determine whether the leak is in the pond, in the stream, or in the waterfall by turning off the pump. If the level in the pond stays constant, the leak is in the stream and waterfall.

PREFORMED WATERFALLS

Rigid units provide a relatively easy way to create a small waterfall, and usually include all the materials (except for the pump) that you need. Rigid units, however, are significantly less natural looking than falls made with flexible liner. Plants that drape over the edge of the unit can help it blend into the landscape. Some rigid waterfalls are available in formal styles, but are difficult to find outside of Europe.

Rigid units come in a variety of finishes, forms, and materials. Some have a natural shape, while others are boldly modern. Most are made of fiberglass, which is resists damage from UV rays. Less costly molded plastic and PVC units are available, but may have a correspondingly shorter life. The units are manufactured as either one-piece models or in designs with several parts that require friction-fit or bolted assembly.

To install a rigid waterfall unit, first mark its outline on the ground and dig a shallow trench with a backward slope into the berm or hill to match the outline. Set the bottom piece (or the entire waterfall of a one-piece unit) in a bed of sifted soil or a mix of fine soil and moist sand. Working from the lowest point to the highest, backfill with the soil/sand mixture. Position each subsequent section, overlapping the section below it and continuing to backfill.

Hide the lower portion of the delivery pipe in a shallow trench alongside the unit. Use a flat rock, plant, or other item to conceal the top of the delivery pipe. For the most natural effect, arrange additional stones around the unit, perhaps scattering some randomly along its edges. Turn on the water and adjust the flow valve to get the right effect. Rigid units usually do best with a very gentle flow.

STREAMS AND WATERFALLS
continued

LAYING STONES IN THE BED

After laying the edging around the water course, the next step is to disguise the liner with bed stones. These are rocks of mixed shapes and sizes that you place on the floor of the stream.

Once you've laid the main bed with small stones, experiment with the position of larger stones. Larger rocks help to hide the liner and help to add splash, sparkle, and movement to the stream when placed where the current flows over and around them. Use rocks in a variety of shapes and sizes, referring to any personal photos or pictures of streams you've clipped from magazines as you planned your water feature.

INSTALLING A STREAM STEP BY STEP

1. EXCAVATION: If necessary, create a berm to give the watercourse the necessary slope. Compact any in-fill soil or let it settle for three months. Mark out the watercourse with stakes and twine. Then begin digging, creating any preplanned pools first, then the stretches of stream.

2. UNDERLAYMENT AND LINER: Install underlayment to prevent tears in the liner. Spread out the flexible liner, positioning and folding it as needed. For larger streams, you will need several sections of liner; overlap the higher sections on each lower one. Seal the seam.

3. PLUMBING: Position the pump in the pond at the opposite end from the waterfall or stream, where it will provide maximum water aeration. Attach the pump to piping in the pond and run it up along the stream to the outlet that you've roughly positioned into place.

4. TESTING: Turn on the pump and check to see how the water flows. Make adjustments by adding or removing soil under the liner.

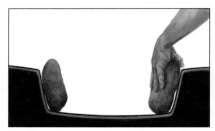

5. EDGING: Lay a rough row of stones along the stream edges. You can mortar the stones to prevent water from flowing under them and being wasted. Trim liner edges.

6. LAYING BED STONE: Disguise the liner with small stones, pebbles, and gravel in the bed. Scatter some among the edging stones, too, for a natural effect. Use as little gravel as possible because it tends to collect algae. Test the flow again.

7. REFINING: With the pump running, experiment with the placement of larger stones to see how they affect sounds and the water's splashing effect. Add or subtract stones as needed or reposition existing stones.

Next, position the water outlet in its permanent location above the top header pool. Disguise it with rocks, soil, and plants. Conceal any piping along the watercourse by burying it under soil or stones.

If a lot of soil or debris has collected in the pond and watercourse as you worked—or if you used muriatic acid to clean the pond—empty the watercourse by either pumping or bailing. Then completely refill it with fresh water.

You can further refine the flow of the watercourse—making it run faster or slower—by turning the flow valve on the pump.

HOW TO CREATE A WATERFALL

A waterfall can be only a small splash down a few rocks into a tiny trough or a trickle on the side of a pond. Or it can be a huge, roaring cascade as part of an extensive stream. A waterfall can work alone or as one of several in a series.

A waterfall that is part of a stream has essentially three parts: the header pool, the lip over which water falls, and the catch basin. Water collects in the header pool then spills over the lip and into the catch basin (which can be a header pool for the next waterfall, if there is one).

When digging a waterfall, create a 12-inch shelf of compacted soil that extends into the streambed to support the weight of the waterfall lip and any stones on it. You can also support the lip with boulders, concrete blocks, bricks, packed mortar, or poured concrete. Install underlayment and liner over the support.

Waterfalls made with larger rocks—a foot or more across—look more natural and are more stable if you prop the lip on a foundation stone: a rectangular piece (or two) set vertically under the lip.

Mini waterfalls have become popular as more gardeners seek small-space features for their landscape. After all, not all waterfalls have to be part of long watercourses that stretch for yards and yards. These designs are very small, taking up less space than a breadbox. You can build them to stand independently in the landscape or position them alongside a pool or pond. However they're designed, they create a charming way to add splash and a cooling effect to your landscape.

To create a mini waterfall on the side of a pool or pond, install flexible piping on the pump. Run the piping to the intended site for the waterfall and arrange a pile of stones 1 or 2 feet high (you may want to build up a small earth mound on which to position them). You can create a lip and foundation stone for the waterfall or you can arrange the stones in any other manner. Turn the pump on periodically to see how the water flows over the stones.

You may want to purchase a preformed mini-waterfall unit. Install it at the side of the pool or pond with its lip slightly overlapping the edge of the pool, then pack loose soil and sand around it. Run the plumbing the same way you would for a stone waterfall.

Create a mini waterfall by laying stones in a "pile." Position one rock, such as this large flat stone, to serve as the waterfall's lip.

Build up the pile further and position flexible tubing attached to a submersible pump in the pond. Adjust the flow to get just the right effect.

LIGHTING

You can create amazing effects with water-feature lighting—make a fountain glow, illuminate an entire pond from within, highlight an attractive statue, or heighten the reflection of a particularly beautiful tree.

HINT

For the best effect when positioning an in-water light to illuminate moving water, make sure the beam shines in the same direction as the water flows.

Water-garden lights are available for installation as either in-water or outside-the-water lighting. All, however, should be connected to a GFI for safety, and those used in the water should be made specifically for underwater use.

Before you shop for water-garden lights, experiment with different effects from a powerful flashlight or a spotlight on an extension cord (never place either in the water). Aim for restraint and subtlety. Don't let yourself get carried away with an effect that's more amusement park than understated elegance.

There are several types of in-water lights, and each creates its own special effect, depending on how you position it (see the box on the opposite page). Most designs call for lights that have dark, subdued casings. Stainless steel or white casings can be obtrusive, especially during daytime.

Fountain lights, either in white or colors, add drama to a spray. Some fountain lights also come equipped with transparent wheels of several colors. Colored light, however, should be used sparingly—it can easily become garish.

Many lights include built-in timers that allow you to automatically turn the lights on and off. You can also install an independent timer in the lighting setup. Timers not only

With a small in-pond light placed behind it, this waterfall comes alive after dark. Lights add hours to the enjoyment of the water feature.

save you the trouble of regulating the light, they also save energy costs.

PLACING LIGHTS

The one rule in placing lights is to never let them shine directly on the water because they will create a harsh glare. In-pond lights need fairly clear water to be effective. Murky water blocks too much light and diminishes the light's effectiveness considerably. If you have fish in your water garden, leave dark areas where they can retreat from the light. Fish need plenty of crevices for refuge. And never light up the entire pond, especially all night.

Whenever possible, position out-of-water lights to conceal their housings and cords: underneath a deck, behind a rock, or tucked into the foliage of a shrub.

Whatever type of lighting you choose, be sensitive to its effect on the neighbors. Don't let the lights shine in their windows.

INSTALLING LOW-VOLTAGE LIGHTING

Unlike regular 120-volt lights, installation of low-voltage landscape lights is a snap, even for beginners. And they're fairly safe because of their low voltage. Many low-voltage lighting systems are sold as kits, complete with instructions.

Hooking up a low-voltage system starts with installing a transformer, which reduces the regular household current from 120 volts to 12 volts. Install the transformer near the GFI receptacle closest to the water feature, following the manufacturer's instructions. Even 12-volt systems should use a GFI unit to prevent shocks. Most transformers are simply mounted next to an outlet and plugged into it.

Run exterior electrical cable from the transformer to the lights. It's important to choose a cable that has the right size of wire for the total wattage of the bulbs in the system (simply add the total watts of each bulb supplied by the cable): #14 wire can handle up to 144 watts, #12 wire up to 192 watts, and #10 wire up to 288 watts.

Bury the cable several inches under the ground, running it through a length of PVC pipe if you want extra protection from tillers and spades.

Then attach the lights to the cable. Some lights attach with clips; others must be wired into the system. Be sure to refer to the instructions that come with the lights.

WATER GARDEN LIGHTS

FLOATING

Drifting on top of the water, floating lights create a festive atmosphere. Some have smoked glass, which has a more subdued effect. To hold the lights in one place, anchor the cord with smooth-edged brick or stone.

SUBMERGED

Made for underwater use, submerged lights illuminate the pool or draw attention to features outside the pool, such as special plants or statues. They also add drama when installed under fountains or waterfalls. Underwater lighting is available for both floodlighting and spotlighting effects, and their lighting is diffused.

FLOODLIGHT

Use the wide beam of a floodlight to illuminate large areas. Inside a pond or pool, it can make the body of water seem to glow from within. Outside the pool, it's best to restrict lighting to a seating area, such as a deck, because it produces a glare if directed at a sharp angle to the water. If used outside the pool position it to shoot across the water at a low angle.

SPOTLIGHT

Whether under or out of the water, the tight beam of a spotlight can shine upward to highlight a specific feature. Place it beneath an attractive element, such as a waterfall, and the element will appear to glow. When carefully positioned under the water, a spotlight can create a reflection of the feature it illuminates. Outside the water, aim it to highlight a feature in the water or place it under statues, trees, or other large poolside plants.

OUT-OF-POOL LIGHTS

Low-voltage lights installed along a path or at the water's edge are called out-of-pond lights. This category includes spotlights, floodlights, and other light fixtures located outside the water.

PLANTING AND STOCKING A GARDEN POOL

Plants and fish put the crowning touches on a water garden. They add greenery, color, and motion to even the smallest and simplest of water features.

First-time water gardeners will be amazed at how quickly a whole new world can grow, literally at their feet—fascinating water plants send roots below the pond surface, exotic lilies float leisurely along the water, fish with elegant ribbonlike fins dart among the depths.

If you're a beginning water gardener, you should start with inexpensive fish and plants during the first year or two. If something dies, you've lost little time and money.

Novice or expert, climate partly determines what plants and fish you can have. Cold-climate gardeners, for example, must make special provisions for tender plants, such as tropical water lilies, and for overwintering fish.

Planning is the key to plant and fish selection. You don't have to chart everything in detail, but when selecting water-garden plants, make a list with an eye for variety—textures, shapes, heights, and colors—just as you would in the landscape at large. Also take into consideration plant sizes at maturity (they might grow larger than you think), as well as how aggressive a plant might be—a problem especially pronounced in water plants.

Novice and experienced gardeners alike will thrill at the discovery of new plants and exotic fish—two new worlds that open up after creating a water garden.

CHOOSING PLANTS

Selecting plants for your first water garden might seem daunting. After all, these are plants unknown to you and you've never grown anything in their environment. But the unknown is a challenge and exciting. Here's some useful information to get you started.

There are four types of water-garden plants. Refer to the encyclopedia of water plants on page 76 as you make your choices. Experiment with one type or try all four. However, if you examine the healthiest unfiltered water gardens, you'd likely find that those with the cleanest water have a mix of floaters, submerged plants, and deep-water aquatic plants.

Water lilies are among the most beautiful of floating water plants and are reason enough to create a water garden.

FLOATERS: As the name implies, these float in the water—their leaves and blossoms on the surface, their roots dangling loose beneath. The floater group, which includes water lettuce, water hyacinth, and duckweed, provides shade and, often, food for fish or wildlife. Some species are natural water filters. Ideally, foliage of floaters and other deep-water plants should cover about half the pond surface to shade the water. If they cover more than two-thirds of the pond, they trap carbon dioxide and other gases in the water. Floaters are easy to grow: Set them in the water, and they take care of themselves. If they get out of control, pull them out by hand or with a net.

WATER LILIES AND OTHER DEEP-WATER PLANTS: Rooted in pots at the bottom of the pond, water lilies and their look-alike cousins, lotuses, send up leaves to float on the surface. They shade the water and keep it cool. There are two kinds of water lilies: tropical and hardy. Tropical water lilies grow from tubers and are profuse bloomers with blossoms that stand on stems above the water surface. Hardy water lilies grow from rhizomes and are somewhat less showy. Their blossoms are smaller and most float on the water surface. Wait until the water has warmed to 70° F before you plant tropicals. Plant hardy varieties when the ice is off the pond.

SUBMERGED PLANTS: Submerged plants, such as water milfoil and hornwort, also grow in pots at the bottom of the pond, but their foliage grows primarily or completely underwater. They are often mistakenly called oxygenators, and some do, in fact, add small amounts of oxygen to the water. They also absorb carbon dioxide and minerals, which inhibit algae growth. Submerged plants provide underwater cover—good spawning areas for fish—and some provide food for the fish, as well. They also help filter the water. Submerged plants are sold in bunches of six stems. Plant one bunch about every 3 square feet. Submerged plants need less soil than water lilies and require a higher proportion of sand or gravel. Don't fertilize submerged plants; they get their nutrients from minerals dissolved in the pond. Mix varieties: Some will do better than others.

MARGINALS: These are shallow-water plants grown in pots on shelves at the edge of the garden pond. Many, such as iris and arrowhead, can double as bog plants. In the water, they're best grown in containers that you can lift for grooming and dividing (splitting into smaller plants when they are overgrown). That will prevent them from becoming invasive.

The function of marginal plants is almost always purely ornamental. They add color and form and help the water garden blend visually into the rest of the landscape. You may want to try putting several plants of one marginal in one large container, but don't mix species in a pot—the strong ones will overtake the weaker.

PLANT PLANNING

When planning for plants, measure the pool's surface area so you can space them correctly. Make rough sketches of your prospective garden pond from various angles and include the location of the plants. Try a variety of

Vigorous parrot's feather creates a striking planting beside water lilies. Many water-garden plants spread rapidly and can take over a garden pool if not maintained properly.

forms, colors, textures, and bloom times. Include trees and other surrounding plants in your sketches to get an overall impression of the impact of your design.

Dry-land design principles apply to ponds. You can use a single large plant as a specimen, but smaller plants in groups of three or more will have the strongest effect. Don't overdo it; water should be the focus of your garden pool. Plants should enhance, not dominate.

Before you buy any plant, find out how well behaved it is. Water-garden plants, especially floaters, have a tendency to be invasive in ideal climates. Some states ban certain water garden species because they clog the natural waterways. Invasive plants also can create a maintenance headache; they'll battle you for control, and you'll spend hours pulling them out of the pool.

Take into account, too, how plants will interact with fish. Duckweed, for example, although invasive, is a favorite food for goldfish and koi. The fish will often eat it rapidly and keep it under control. Koi and some other fish are boisterous and will uproot and shred plants.

Water movement is another element to plan for. Deep-water aquatics, especially water lilies and other floaters, prefer water that is nearly or completely still. Other plants thrive in fast-moving currents. Still others do well in either. A fountain can push floaters away with its splashing or it may wet their leaves, which many plants don't like.

The hardiness of a perennial plant (its ability to survive winter cold) can often be extended by simply lowering it below the expected ice depth in autumn. If you live where winter temperatures reach minus 20° F, for example, plants hardy to minus 10° F may thrive if you set them deep enough.

HINT

In still water, position floating plants around potted marginals. They'll help block the view of the pots for a more natural look.

GROWING WATER GARDEN PLANTS

Submerged plants
Place on pond bottom

Bricks and other supports
Use to adjust heights as needed

Marginal and bog plants
Provide a special shelf in shallow water

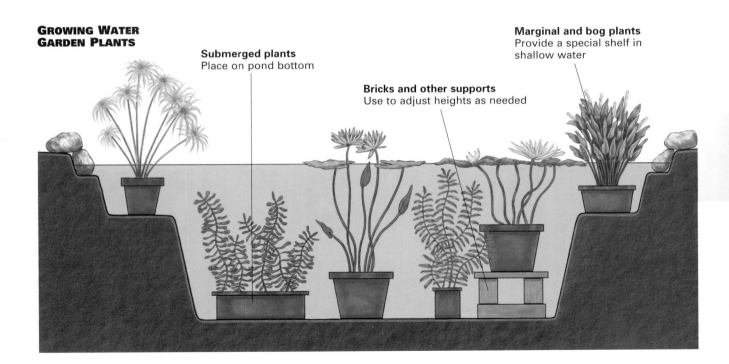

PLANTING AND CARING FOR POTTED WATER PLANTS

While plants in natural ponds root in the mud on the bottom of the pond, those in garden ponds (except floaters) thrive in pots.

Most are potted in the same way as terrestrial plants, then set gently in the pool. You can introduce them into the pond immediately after filling it, following the precautions on page 21.

Choices for pots are numerous. You can use a regular black plastic pot, which blends into the background, but there are also aquatic baskets that have a large open weave. Line these with burlap, landscape fabric, or a woven plastic made for ponds before using.

The size of the container is determined by the needs of the plant. A vigorous water lily, for example, requires a container that's about 16 inches across. Most marginals can survive in an 8- to 10-inch pot. Tall plants may need broader pots to keep the wind from tipping them over. Small containers should have a ballast—a brick in the bottom of the pot works well.

The number of plants you can fit into a container is also plant dependent. Each lily, for example, should grow in its own basket so the pattern of its leaves shows off at their best. Many submerged plants, on the other hand, do well squeezed four or five in a 10-inch pot. Use your best judgment, but always err on the side of too much room in the container.

Pot water plants in high-quality topsoil or in a potting soil made specifically for water gardens. Don't use potting soils with peat or perlite; these materials float out of the container (ask the retailer if a brand you're considering contains these ingredients). Peat also increases the acidity of the water. Avoid potting soil that contains fertilizer. After planting, top the soil with pea gravel to hold it down and prevent it from floating out.

Caring for water plants isn't the same as tending their landlocked cousins. You still need to plant, fertilize, and groom them, but in a slightly different way.

SETTING THE DEPTH

To position plants at just the right depth, set their containers on a stack of weathered exterior bricks. Or place them on black plastic storage boxes (buy the milk-crate type with grid or mesh sides so they don't float).

When planting water lilies and other deep-water aquatics, some gardeners immediately place the container at its permanent depth. Others believe deep-water plants do better if they are gradually lowered into the water as they grow so their leaves are always afloat. To pursue the second strategy, remove a brick or two as the stems grow, continuing until the pot rests at the proper depth of about 2 feet.

EASY DOES IT

Placing a container in the center of a large water feature is easy if the plants are in pots with handles. Run twine or rope through the handles, and set the container near the water's edge. Recruit a friend to help, then each of you take an end of the rope and stand on opposite sides of the pond. Lower the plant gently into place and pull out the cord.

TIDY UP

As your plants grow, trim off any dead or diseased plant matter. Carefully deadhead (cut off) spent flowers to promote continued blooming, to prevent disease, and to

keep the water garden tidy. Skim out floaters that cover too much surface area of the pool. Established submerged plants may have to be thinned by raking out the overgrowth every few weeks. Or lift the pot and trim off some stems. Net leaves, grass clippings, and other debris every day or so to prevent them from decaying and fouling the water.

FERTILIZING AND DISEASE

Once established, water garden plants benefit from fertilizing. But regular fertilizers can be toxic to fish and can encourage algae. Use aquatic fertilizer instead; it's sold as large pellets, which you push into the soil. Aquatic fertilizer is available at garden centers or through mail-order companies (see "Garden Pool Resources" on page 91).

You can prevent many plant pests (both insects and diseases) by choosing plants suited to your climate, by practicing proper water-garden care, and by maintaining a balanced ecosystem. Fish and frogs, for example, are helpful because they eat many insect pests.

The incidence of disease in water plants is small, but when disease does strike, select a product specifically labeled for use around water gardens. Some pesticides throw off the balance of the pond and promote algae and other problems. Others are toxic to fish.

DIVISION

In your second and subsequent years of water gardening, your plants may crowd their pots or become rampant; if so, they need division. You'll know by the signs: reduced bloom and congested crowns in which older foliage crowds out young stems and leaves. Marginals may show dead roots around the crown. Water lily tubers might overgrow the top of the pot or fill it so tightly they distort its shape.

To divide plants that grow from rhizomes, remove them from their pots and break the plant into several pieces. Repot each piece having a growing tip. Plants with runners or plantlets can usually be divided by breaking off the "baby" plant.

HINT

You don't need to use special aquatic containers for planting. Those black plastic pots that regular nursery plants come in are fine—and free.

PLANTING IN A CONTAINER

You can plant all water-garden plants (except floaters) in black plastic pots and place them at various levels of the pool or pond. There are containers made specifically for water planting, but the regular plastic pots you get at the nursery work just as well.

To pot the plant, remove it from its original container. It's a good idea to rinse off the plant to wash away any insects. Partially fill the pot with good-quality potting soil (avoid those containing peat, perlite, or fertilizers) and gently position the plant in its new pot. Tropical water lilies should be set in the center of the container, while hardy water lilies should be set at the edge of the pot. Make sure the plant is at the same level it was in its original container. Add additional plants if there is room in the container, and fill the pot with soil (leave about a half inch below the rim). Now is a good time to pinch off any damaged or yellow leaves.

Spread a layer of pea or dark gravel on top of the soil to keep it from floating out of the container and to help it blend into the background of the pond bottom.

Position the plant in the pond at the correct level. To raise a plant, stack a few weathered bricks underneath it or put the pot on a black plastic storage crate. With some plants, you may need to get into the pool—a job you can do in your bare feet or in wader boots.

ENCYCLOPEDIA OF WATER PLANTS

DEEP-WATER PLANTS
HARDY WATER LILIES
(*Nymphaea* spp.) These beauties are able to withstand colder temperatures than their tropical cousins and can overwinter as long as the rhizome remains below ice level. They don't do well, however, when water temperatures exceed 95° F for prolonged periods. They are somewhat less showy than tropicals, tend not to have an intense fragrance, and no night-blooming or blue varieties exist. Flowers bloom in white, pink, yellow, peach, or red from spring through fall, depending on cultivar. Plant spread varies from 2–12 square feet. Plant crowns 8–24 inches below the water surface. They need calm water and prefer full sun, but will tolerate partial shade. Zones 4–10.

TROPICAL DAY-BLOOMING
WATER LILIES (*Nymphaea* spp.) These profuse bloomers come in a wide variety of colors—even blue—and have a heavy fragrance and luxurious foliage. They hold their large, showy blossoms up on tall stems several inches above the water and make good cut flowers. Each bloom opens midmorning, closes in late afternoon, and lasts about four days. As their name suggests, they bloom during daylight. Some varieties spread up to 5 feet. Plant them 4–12 inches below the water surface. Day bloomers prefer sun and flourish in hot weather. They must not be in water cooler than 70° F. Bring them indoors during winter in most parts of the country; they are winter hardy only in zones 10–11.

TROPICAL NIGHT-BLOOMING
WATER LILIES (*Nymphaea* spp.) Night bloomers share the same characteristics as their day-blooming relatives, but open their blossoms in early evening and keep them open through midmorning, longer if they're not hit with early-morning sun or if the air temperature remains cool. Their evening show is valued, especially by gardeners who can't often be in their gardens during the day. They tend to have an even sweeter fragrance than their day-blooming cousins. Plant these tropical night bloomers 4–12 inches below the water surface. They thrive in intense sun but are highly sensitive to frost and dislike cool weather. Tropical night-blooming water lilies are hardy in zones 10–11.

DWARF OR MINIATURE WATER
LILIES (*Nymphaea* spp.) Dwarf species share qualities with other water lilies but they spread to only 1–2 feet. They are an excellent choice for the very small pond or container water garden. Their flowers are smaller, also, just 1–5 inches across (notice the penny in the photograph). For their size, they are fairly prolific bloomers, sometimes producing two to three dozen flowers at one time. This bloom quantity, however, is less than their larger cousins. Mini water lilies come in fewer colors than full-sized water lilies. Plant dwarf water lilies 4–10 inches below the surface of the water. They are hardy generally in zones 4–11, but their hardiness will vary from cultivar to cultivar.

LOTUSES
(*Nelumbo* spp.) Lotuses have large, exotic flowers with unusual centers, which can be used in dried flower arrangements. Blooms spread up to 6 inches across. The flower stalks rise up to 5 feet above floating leaves. Flowers are intensely fragrant, can perfume an entire corner of the garden, and are available in many colors. Miniature varieties of lotuses—bowl lotus—are becoming popular. They have flower stalks that grow just 1–3 feet above the water surface. Plant lotuses in full sun with their crowns 2–12 inches below the surface of the water. They'll need several weeks with temperatures of 80° F or higher to bloom well. Lotuses are hardy in zones 4–11. Like dwarf water lilies, their hardiness will vary from cultivar to cultivar.

SUBMERGED PLANTS

CANADIAN PONDWEED (*Elodea canadensis*) The tiny, deep green to reddish-green, fern-like leaves on pondweed's delicate whorling branches create ideal cover for spawning fish. Fish also eat the foliage, especially during winter. Pondweed quickly regrows. Growth, in fact, can be too vigorous, and the plants may need thinning with a rake. One of the best and most reliable of the submerged plants, pondweed competes with algae for food. Plant it 6 inches to 5 feet below the water surface, depending on water clarity. Full sun is best but it will tolerate some shade. Weight the pot with small stones to keep it on the bottom. Zones 4–10.

HORNWORT (*Ceratophyllum demersum*) Also called coontail, the slender stems of hornwort grow up to 2 feet long and carry whorls of feathery, densely forked leaves. The effect of the stems and leaves is like a bottlebrush. Hornwort tolerates more shade and deeper water than many other submerged plants, and it is one of the most recommended plants for water gardens. It is easily kept under control. In the summer, it is rootless and usually floats free in the water. It anchors itself on the bottom during winter. Plant it 2–4 inches below the water surface in sun or shade. Hornwort is hardy in zones 4–10.

CURLED PONDWEED (*Potamogeton crispus*) The narrow, translucent, stalkless leaves of curled pondweed have wavy edges that resemble seaweed. Each leaf grows to about 3 inches long, but its stems can grow disproportionally long—up to 13 feet—so its use is generally restricted to larger water gardens. Small, pink-tinged flowers appear in spring. Curled pondweed can be invasive in some situations, so you may have to watch it carefully. It does best in a pond with moving water rather than in a still pond. It will tolerate cloudy water. You can plant it as deep as 3 feet. The best site for it is in full sun to partial shade. Curled pondweed is hardy in zones 4–10.

CABOMBA (*Cabomba caroliniana*) Also called fanwort, cabomba leaves vary with the species. Most have bright green underwater foliage of graceful fans and tiny white flowers in summer. The foliage is an ideal environment for spawning and a good hideout for baby fish. Plants does best in cool water up to 30 inches deep. Avoid planting in shallow water or in raised pools, where water is warm. Cabomba grows up to 8 inches long. Plant it in coarse, sandy soil 2 inches deep and submerge under 1 foot of water. It likes filtered light but tolerates part shade and full sun. Plants are hardy in zones 5–10, depending on species.

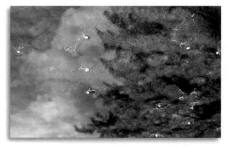

WATER MILFOIL (*Myriophyllum* spp.) Water milfoil has long, trailing stems that grow from 6 to 20 feet long with tufts of fine, feathery foliage in green or brown. It provides good spawning areas for fish and is a good plant for trapping debris. Its stems extend above the surface with spikes of tiny, pale yellow flowers. Some varieties produce flowers on the water surface. They sway attractively in moving water. Water milfoil does well in shallow water or small ponds. Plant it 12–30 inches below the water surface in full sun to partial shade or filtered light. It is hardy in zones 4–11, depending on the species.

WILD CELERY (*Vallisneria americana*) Also called ribbon, eel or tape grass, wild celery has lovely, ribbon-like leaves that reach 1 to 3 feet long. They sway with the movement of the water. 'Spiralis' is a dwarf cultivar that grows to only 8 inches tall. Wild celery is tolerant of warm water, and it will spreads to form a pleasant carpet across the surface of the water. You'll find that it is an excellent source of food and shelter for fish. The plants produce greenish flowers all season long, and they are an ideal natural filter for the garden pool. Plant wild celery in water that is 12–24 inches deep. It will grow in shade to full sun, and it is hardy in zones 4–11.

ENCYCLOPEDIA OF WATER PLANTS
continued

MARGINALS

PARROT'S FEATHER
(Myriophyllum aquaticum. Also listed as *M. proserpinacoides)* This plant's pink stems trail silvery blue or lime-green foliage. Its flowers are insignificant. Leaves are sparse underwater. However, about 6 inches above the surface, they grow into feathery whorls. Parrot's feather is good for trailing over the side of a container water garden or alongside a waterfall. It is a fast-growing marginal plant and may need to be thinned occasionally. To survive cold winters, plants must be under ice. Plant their crowns 4–10 inches below the water surface. Parrot's feather likes full sun but tolerates partial shade. It is adapted to hardiness zones 3–11.

IRIS
Marginal species of iris include blue or wild flag iris *(I. versicolor,* lovely blue, bearded flowers); rabbitear iris *(I. laevigata,* usually white, broad-petaled, beardless flowers); Louisiana iris *(I. fulva,* red to orange beardless blossoms); and Japanese water iris *(I. ensata,* also called *I. kaempferi,* white, blue, purple, reddish-purple and lavender-pink beardless blooms). Another, yellow flag iris *(I pseudacorus,* beardless), is especially easy to grow. *I. laevigata* 'Variegata' is popular for its striped leaves. All these irises also grow well in bog conditions. Plant iris rhizomes (the fleshy, rootlike portion) 2–4 inches below the water surface in full sun to light shade. They are hardy in zones 2–10, depending on the species.

ARROWHEAD *(Sagittaria* spp.)
This marginal is named for its arrowhead-shaped leaves that rise up 1–2 feet above the surface of the water on slender stems. Because of these slender stems, the plant may flop a little. Some species have narrow leaves; others have broad leaves. Three species are grown as garden-pool marginals: *S. sagittifolia, S. latifolia,* and *S. japonica.* Arrowhead blooms later than most other marginals; its white flowers emerge in summer. It is a North American native plant. Although easy to grow, arrowhead doesn't transplant well, and it recovers slowly after moving. It grows well in boggy conditions. Plant its roots 1–5 inches beneath the water surface in full sun to partial shade. Plants are hardy in zones 4–10.

MARSH MARIGOLD
(Caltha palustris) One of the most popular marginals, marsh marigold's bright golden spring flowers bloom above heart-shaped, shiny, dark green leaves for a month or more. The plants rise about 1 foot above the water and spread about a foot across. They go dormant by midsummer. Grow them near other marginals to ensure that the bare spot they leave are hidden by their neighbor's foliage. Marsh marigolds are a good choice to plant in damp spots near a stream, and they grow well in bog gardens. They are native to North America. Plant marsh marigold in full sun so its crown is no deeper than 2 inches below the surface of the water. Plants are hardy in zones 4–10.

CATTAIL *(Typha* spp.)
The familiar brown flower heads of cattail are borne in late summer through early fall. Many species are too invasive to grow in garden pools, but there are few species that you can plant without fear of them taking over. For large water gardens, there's *T. latifolia; T. laxmannii* is suitable for gardens of medium size, and the miniature cattail, *T. minima,* does fine in small garden ponds. Growing cattails in pots helps to keep them from getting out of hand. Cattail plants can grow up to 4 feet tall, depending on the species. Plant them so that their crowns are up to 4 inches below the water surface. The plants grow best in full sun to partial shade. Cattails are hardy in zones 2–10, depending on the species.

FLOATING PLANTS

WATER LETTUCE (*Pistia stratiotes*)
Also called shellflower, its deeply creased, lime-green leaves form heads resembling lettuce. Water lettuce spreads by plantlets that break off from the mother plant. Mature plants can stretch 6 inches across and form a colony several feet wide by summer's end. Growing it is prohibited in some states because it can become a nuisance. Easy to grow in most climates, water lettuce can be tricky in cool water and low humidity. Plant it in partial shade for the best color and growth; it will tolerate slightly deeper shade and full sun. Treat water lettuce as an annual in most parts of country. It is hardy only in zones 9–10.

WATER HYACINTH (*Eichhornia crassipes*) Water hyacinth produces lovely blue midsummer blossoms on short, about 8-inch spikes that grow above shiny, rounded leaves. It spreads rapidly and is invasive in warm parts of the country. It is banned in some areas because it can take over portions of natural waterways. It is, however, killed completely by light frost. Its trailing roots make good spawning grounds for fish. It is an outstanding water filter. Water hyacinth likes full sun and is treated as an annual in most parts of the country. It is winter hardy only in zones 9–10.

DUCKWEED (*Lemna* spp.) This is a vigorous plant with thin, tiny, angular, or cloverlike leaves that hang just below the water surface. It is an excellent food for goldfish and koi. Duckweed shades the water surface well, and it tends to thin out slightly in summer's hottest weather. Ivy-leaf duckweed (*L. trisulca*) is the smallest-leafed and least invasive. Skim out excess regularly in small ponds. Avoid other varieties. *L. minor*, for example, is very prolific and is found in stagnant natural ponds everywhere. Thick duckweed (*L. gibba*) and greater duckweed (*Spirodela polyrrhiza*) are also very invasive. Duckweed has a broad range of hardiness, growing well in zones 2–11.

FAIRY MOSS (*Azolla* spp.) Also called water fern, this is one of the most widely available floaters. Its tiny fronds, about ½ inch across, spread rapidly and form dense, pale green clusters, which goldfish feed on. The fronds turn red in summer. Fairy moss can be invasive, so is best used in ponds where it is possible to control it by regular netting. Although it is hardy to zone 7, it will die if the water freezes. In colder areas, save some in a jar filled with water and soil, and reintroduce it to the pool in spring. *A. caroliniana* is the variety usually offered. It grows in sun to partial shade and is hardy in zones 7–10.

SALVINIA (*Salvinia rotundifolia*)
Also called water or butterfly fern, the leaves of these tiny plants form layers of ruffles along the length of the stems. The small, floating leaves are pale green or purplish-brown and covered with fine, silky hairs. Salvinia grows in large, floating colonies; it can become somewhat invasive. However, you can keep it from getting out of hand in small ponds by thinning out the plants with regular netting. Plan on a heavy thinning early in the summer because salvinia particularly thrives in hot, sunny conditions and will get out of control then. In most regions, water gardeners use salvinia as an annual because it is hardy only in zones 10–11.

FROGBIT (*Hydrocharis morsus-ranae*) Its tiny flowers (about ½ inch across) resemble a small, white, papery water lily. Frogbit leaves are kidney-shaped, veined, shiny, and about 1 inch across. The foliage dies back in autumn and the plants survive as dormant buds on the bottom. Growth begins again in early summer. Frogbit spreads by runners, but its growth is restrained. It likes calm, shallow water about a foot deep, and it may root in mud. You can overwinter the buds in a jar filled with water and soil, replanting them in spring. This plant likes full sun. An annual in cold-winter areas, it is hardy in zones 7–10.

FISH

GALLERY OF FISH

RED COMET
A relatively new type of goldfish, red comets boast elegantly long fins and tail. They feed at all levels and are hardy, tolerating water as cool as 39° F and as warm as 95° F, but not for long periods at either extreme.

CALICO FANTAIL
Calico fantails are similar to comets but have a more egg-shaped body and an even larger double tail. Their scales can appear metallic or pearly. Calico fantails tolerate temperatures of 55° to 70° F. They are sensitive to prolonged low temperatures.

SHUBUNKINS
Often called calico goldfish, shubunkins are popular and easy to care for. They come in many colors, including blue. Several varieties are available, including London, which has a calico pattern on a striking blue background. Bristol shubunkins have the same pattern as Londons, and also have pearly scales and a large, forked tail with rounded ends. Shubunkins grow to 10 inches and are hardy, tolerating temperatures between 39° and 85° F.

KOI
Though choice koi are costly, not all are expensive. They grow to about 2 feet, are hearty eaters, especially of plants, and need a large pond with a good filtration system to dispose of their considerable waste. They can be boisterous enough to knock over pots. Koi feed at all levels and breed easily. They prefer cool 39° to 68° F temperatures.

COMMON GOLDFISH
Usually orange-red, the common goldfish feeds at all water levels. Most grow less than 10 inches long, are easily bred, and may live for 10 years or more. They prefer a weedy pond with a muddy bottom. Hardy, they will tolerate water as cool as 39° F and as warm as 95° F, though neither extreme for long periods.

Fish add sparkle and movement to a water garden like nothing else. Before you stock your pond, however, there are a number of things to consider.

First, check the water. Ask your supplier what chemicals the water contains. It's likely that it has either chlorine or chloramines, or both. You can remove chlorine with a dechlorinator or let it dissipate by allowing the water to sit for a few days (several weeks is better, not only to remove chlorine but to establish plants for cover and food for the fish). Chloramines must be removed with a chloramine remover. You can introduce fish to the water within 20 minutes of adding either a dechlorinator or chloramine remover.

CLIMATE AND CONDITIONS

Plan fish purchases with your climate and your pond size in mind. Most fish do best in large ponds because water temperatures and oxygen levels are more stable in larger volumes of water. Some fish, however, do well only in cool water, others prefer warmth, and still others tolerate both extremes.

As a rule, the smaller the pond, the more tolerant of temperature extremes your fish must be. Water heats and cools with ambient temperatures; larger ponds are slower to respond to the changes so the temperature is consistent. For that reason, a pond that is more than 3 feet deep, can house fish with a narrow tolerance for temperature change. But fish in a small pond containing just 50 to 75 gallons, or less as in a container garden, must be able to take extremes of both heat and cold. A whiskey barrel half, for example, is adequate for one or two fish—as long as you choose species that aren't finicky about temperature.

Different fish do best at different depths. Koi, for example, need plenty of space in water at least 2 feet deep, but orfe spend most of their time in the upper levels of a pond.

The ideal stocking time is late spring or early summer when the water reaches about 50° F. Although you can stock nearly any kind of fish in your pond, those bred for outdoor conditions will require less care and will generally do better in garden ponds.

WHAT TO LOOK FOR

Most tropical fish centers carry a variety of goldfish, koi, and other varieties. Fish vary considerably in appearance, cost, and care. Common goldfish are a favorite and are easy to keep, but there are more exotic—and more costly—fish available. There are oranda, which cover their heads with a "hood" and egg-shaped moors with telescopic eyes that

HINT

Before introducing fish to your pond, quarantine them for two weeks in a separate aerated aquarium or container to ensure they are disease and parasite free.

Fish add movement to a garden pool and are as beautiful as even the most brilliantly colored plant. Some can be trained to come to a certain spot for daily feedings.

protrude from supports. Koi is a favorite of breeders and is even shown in competitions.

If possible, hand-pick your fish to make sure they're healthy. They should be young, preferably not over 3 to 5 inches long, with bright eyes, a sturdy body, and a lively habit. They should swim effortlessly with erect fins and have no damaged or missing scales. Choose several small fish instead of a mixture of large and small varieties; small fish quickly become food for larger companions.

BRINGING THEM HOME

Transport the fish in a plastic bag inside a box. Cover the box so light won't stress the fish. If the fish will be in the bag for more than 4 hours, ask the dealer to add oxygen to the bag. Even with oxygen added, don't leave fish in a sealed bag for more than 36 hours.

Acclimate the fish to the pool by adding about 10 percent pool water to the bag four times every 15 minutes. After putting them in the pond, don't feed the fish for the first three or four days. Then, as they settle in, feed them daily, but never more than what they can eat in 10 to 15 minutes. Excess food will pollute the water. Most fish supplement their diets in the summer with plants, mosquito larvae, and gnats so you can reduce or eliminate summer feedings.

Fish will need shade and cover in the pool. Provide it with plants or bricks, stone, and other materials placed on the bottom or shelves of the pond. You should also equip the pond with a UV clarifier.

If your fish are hardy (hardiness varies, but single-tailed varieties are hardiest), they can overwinter in the deep zone of the pond, which shouldn't freeze. They'll live off their fat reserves. All hardy fish can survive temperatures as low as 39° F as long as there's open water at all times for oxygen to enter and gases to escape. An electric water heater will thaw the ice to provide an opening.

Bring inside tropical fish and fish in pools that freeze solid when temperatures drop to 60° F. Keep them in an aerated aquarium or tub. In spring, after water temperatures reach 50° F, reintroduce them to the pond. Resume feeding hardy fish that wintered in the pool.

HOW MANY FISH?

To calculate the number of fish you can have in your garden pool, figure the total surface area of the water feature in which fish will be present. See page 22 for formulas. (This will give you an indication of how much oxygen will be available to them.) Don't count areas with marginal plants in the total but do include the area covered by floating plants.

As a rule of thumb, each inch of fish should have 6 square inches to 1 square foot of water. (Koi, however, need much more space—about 25 square feet for every fish.) Always err on the side of too much space. Use the table below to help you stock your pond.

2-inch fish: 1 square foot
4-inch fish: 2 square feet
6-inch fish: 3 square feet
8-inch fish: 4 square feet
12-inch fish: 6 square feet
16-inch fish: 12 square feet

If you provide aeration in the form of a fountain, you can add a few more fish. If you have a waterfall, which aerates the water substantially, you may be able to double the number of fish.

MAINTAINING YOUR GARDEN POOL

A well-designed water garden should take minimal time to maintain. Unless you have a very large water feature, you'll spend about an hour or less each week to feed fish, groom plants and monitor water quality. When estimating the amount of time to budget for garden pool maintenance, 10 minutes per thousand gallons of water is a good rule of thumb.

Completely emptying and cleaning the water feature on a regular basis isn't necessary, nor is it advisable. Frequent emptying and cleaning can upset the pond's fragile ecological balance. At most, water gardens need a thorough cleaning only once every three or four years.

If you find that caring for your water garden is taking too much time, it may have a fundamental problem in its design or construction or in the ecological balance of plants, fish, and water. It's better to correct the basic problem instead of spending hours each week fixing its side effects. In the long run, you'll save time and money. If you can't determine the cause of the underlying problem, consider a consultation with a professional water-garden designer.

As long as the pond has no problems, you'll have a burst of chores in the spring and fall and just a little grooming each week in between. The rest of the time is yours— sit back and enjoy the fruits of your hard work.

This entry bridge, left, crosses a courtyard pond where colorful koi gather for hand feeding. Water lilies like this one look delicate but are actually easy to grow.

A BALANCED ECOSYSTEM

In all but the simplest water features, the clarity of water and the health of the plants and fish depend on a balanced ecosystem. Ponds in the wild and garden pools alike contain a complex network of checks and balances that generally maintain the pond's condition without external help.

If your pond is out of balance, it will give you numerous signals: bad smells, fish dying or gasping for breath at the water surface, dark or green water, as well as stunted and diseased plants.

Here's how to keep your garden pool's ecosystem in balance.

■ **USE ALL THE ELEMENTS.** Plants, fish, and other pond life—in water that is well aerated and maintained—work together. All of them, in the right mix, will keep your pond in prime condition.

Floating plants provide shade, cool and filter the water, and control algae. Submerged plants are also filters, and they feed fish as well as create shelter and spawning areas for them. Fish control mosquitoes (they consume the larvae) and will control the algae, too. Snails, also, have voracious appetites for algae.

Stock fish and plants in appropriate proportions to each other and to pond size. Experiment until the balance is right. As a rule, a 6- by 8-foot pond can handle no more than 16 fish (3- to 5-inch), six water snails (such as great pond or ramshorn), and 15 bunches of submerged plants.

■ **KNOW YOUR WATER.** Invest in a kit for water testing. They're inexpensive and a number of types are available. Test for ammonia and nitrite levels when you first fill your pond and then periodically thereafter, particularly if fish are dying.

A careful balancing of plants and fish, as well as regular water garden maintenance will keep your pond sparkling.

Snails may be tiny but they make a big contribution to the pond. They love algae. Most likely, snails will show up in your pool on their own. Otherwise, you can purchase them from a water garden supplier.

If you do have a chemical problem, a partial water change, described below, can help lower ammonia and nitrite levels.

■ **KEEP IT FILLED.** Don't let the pond evaporate—a drop of an inch or more below its normal water level starts to create unhealthy concentrations of salts and minerals and exposes the liner to deteriorating UV rays.

When you add water, fill the pond with just a trickle from the hose (keep it at the bottom of the pond) to allow fish and other pond life to adapt to the gradual changes in temperature and pH. Don't add more than 10 to 20 percent of the total volume at any one time or the fish could go into shock.

■ **PARTIALLY CHANGE THE WATER WHEN NEEDED.** Although it's best to keep the pool filled, over time—even with refills—salt and waste materials build up in the water.

To freshen it, drain the pond by about 10 percent of its capacity (preferably by drawing water from the bottom where concentrations of harmful substances are highest). Then refill it. It's best to do this right before a rain so rainfall can replace at least some of the water. (Never work around your garden pond if there's a threat of lightning.)

Water from a hose is also acceptable as long as you add it slowly with the hose placed at the bottom of the pond and add no more than 20 percent fresh water by volume.

■ **PROVIDE AERATION.** Whether from a fountain or waterfall, splashing water keeps the water well oxygenated, and that's essential for supporting fish. Oxygenated water also stays fresh, warding off foul-smelling bacteria that thrive in a low-oxygen environment.

CONTROLLING ALGAE

One of the most common signs of imbalance in a water garden is free-floating algae, which makes the water green and murky. In severe cases, algae can coat and choke out other plants. It can also stress the fish.

Certain kinds of algae are good for ponds, however. Smooth algae, for example, grows on the liner and on pots. It is a sign of a healthy pond and gives a water garden an attractive patina, making it look as though it has been there a while. In fact, smooth algae growth is called a passive filter because it removes nutrients that feed other, less desirable, algae.

Filamentous and tufted algae (sometimes called blanketweed or string algae), as well as floating phytoplankton algae, are not desirable. These grow in long, dark green, ropey colonies.

All garden ponds, especially during the first two to three weeks after they're constructed or cleaned, have excess algae. Most will have an algae bloom each spring, too, as the pond struggles to reestablish its balance. But as your floating plants grow and begin to shade the water and compete with the algae for light, the water should clear.

Fish are useful in your fight against algae because they eat some of the invasive varieties. Pond snails, which you can buy from a water garden supplier or through the mail, also are voracious algae eaters.

Algae grows rapidly in warm, stagnant water, so keep your pond filled, particularly in hot weather. Deep ponds warm up more slowly than shallow pools.

Filamentous algae, which looks like floating seaweed, should be removed from the surface of the water by hand or with a rake. If it forms on rocks or waterfalls, turn off

the pump and let the algae dry. Then you can scrape and brush it off.

If that doesn't work, rewet the algae and sprinkle it with non-iodized table salt, such as pickling and canning salt. Leave for several hours then brush off. Salt, as long as it is used only rarely and in moderation, kills the algae, but doesn't harm fish.

Use algaecides as a last resort. They stunt the plant growth necessary for a good garden-pool balance.

If algae occurs on a regular basis, a biological filter (see page 26) may be in order for your pool. You might also consider adding a UV clarifier (see page 26), which not only defends your pond from algae, but also destroys many bacteria, viruses, and fungi that could harm the fish.

If you don't have a fountain, or if it's not strong enough to aerate the water and the fish are gulping for air at the surface, add a pump with an air stone on the bottom of the pond.

■ **KEEP THE POND FREE OF LEAVES AND DEBRIS.** Debris decomposes, and if not removed, it fouls the water. Skim leaves, fallen petals, and other floating plant matter from the bottom and surface of the pool with a net. (In a very small water feature, you can probably do this by hand.)

Pinch off yellowing and dying leaves; they can turn into pollutants if left unattended. If tree leaves are a problem in autumn, put a net over the pool to catch them or make skimming the pond a daily routine.

In late fall, when you remove the pump for the winter, make sure the water is free of debris before the pond ices over.

■ **KEEP IT UNDER CONTROL.** If fish numbers get out of hand, give some away. Thin invasive plants regularly and divide overgrown plants so that no one element begins to take over.

■ **CONSIDER A FILTER.** If the garden pool has continuing problems with debris, too much light, or excessive fish waste, consider adding a biological filter to the pool setup. See page 26 for more information on filters.

■ **AVOID MISAPPLICATION OF FERTILIZER AND PESTICIDES.** When fertilizing or applying other chemicals around your garden pool, take care that the materials don't get into the water. Some are toxic to fish, and others can promote algae growth in the water.

■ **FEED FISH PROPERLY.** Feed fish only what they can devour in about 10 minutes. Don't feed them unless they are ravenous.

In hot weather, don't worry if the fish don't seem to be eating much. In summer, they'll get food from other sources: insects and plants. Feeding fish too much or too often will foul the water and create a need for a larger filter.

HINT

Don't be concerned if a whole host of insects comes to visit your pond. Many are beneficial and all are part of the ecological system. Diving water beetles, for example, feast on mosquito larvae.

CLEANING THE POOL

Cleaning a pond is a chore you'll need to perform only once in a while, but it can help keep a pond in balance. Cleaning reduces certain kinds of algae and other pond problems.

Pools need cleaning no more than every three or four years, and large ponds need it even less often. Signs that your pond should be cleaned include overgrown plants and a several-inches thick layer of decomposing debris on the bottom of the pond.

Late summer is the best time to clean a pond in most regions because plants need time to recover before winter hits. In warmer climates, wait until plants go dormant. Before you start, you may want to invest in a pair of waterproof boots or waders, depending on the size of your pond.

To clean the pond, start by draining it. If you have a submersible pump, disconnect the output piping and replace it with a hose run out of the pond and pump out the water. Don't do this with an external pump. It could damage the pump. Siphon out the water, or rent a pump to drain it. You can bail water out of a small pond.

If you have fish, empty enough water from the pool to make it easier to catch them. Net the fish and put them in a bucket or wading pool filled with some of the water from the pond. Set the containers in the shade or take them indoors to a cool room. Cover containers so fish won't jump out. If the fish are going to be in the containers for more than an hour, add an air pump with an air stone to the container.

Continue to remove water until only several inches remain in the bottom of the

pool. Then stop pumping and check the muck for any remaining small fish and beneficial animals, such as frogs or tadpoles. Put these in a bucket also.

Next, remove plants. If the pond cleaning will take more than a couple of hours, wrap their containers and foliage in wet newspaper and put them in a shady place (you can also set them in several inches of water in a wading pool). Put floaters and submerged plants in buckets. Bail the remaining water, and pour it onto flower beds and the rest of the landscape (it will clog drains). Be careful not to damage the liner. Dump mud on a compost heap.

Once the pond is empty, hose it down. Never brush or scrub the liner because that might damage the liner and will also remove beneficial bacteria and helpful algae. After hosing down the pool, remove the dirty water.

Fill the pond about halfway. Add the plants. (If any of them are aggressive, now is a good time to divide them.) Remember to rest the smaller deep-water aquatics on bricks so their leaves can float.

Prepare the water for fish in the same way as for the pool's first stocking. Let chlorine dissipate or add a dechlorinator. Also add chloramine remover, if necessary. Check the fish for disease. Treat them accordingly, then gently place them in the pool in a plastic bag (see page 81). Position the pump, fill the pond, and plug in the pump.

HINT

The last bit of silt and water is more easily removed with a small plastic dustpan.

WINTER CARE

In regions with mild winters, care of the garden pond consists of little more than an occasional check on the pond and its inhabitants. However, in colder parts of the country, you'll need to protect the water feature itself as well as its inhabitants.

First, the water feature. Pools made of concrete, brick, masonry, tile, or other porous material can crack. If there's any danger of a pool freezing solid, where the entire depth of water turns to ice, drain it using a pump or siphon hose. Also drain ponds made from rigid liner and wall or freestanding fountains. Ponds made from flexible plastic liner or natural clay-lined ponds don't need to be drained.

Instead of draining the pool, you can install a stock tank deicer to keep it from freezing. However, deicers can be expensive to operate, costing as much as $100 a month in electricity in some areas.

In regions where air temperatures don't drop below minus 10° F, use an air pump with an air stone to keep the water moving enough to prevent freezing. Where temperatures stay above minus 20° F, a water pump will keep the pool from freezing solid. Both of these methods, however, work best in ponds holding 1,000 gallons or more because large bodies of water freeze more slowly than smaller ones.

In mild climates where ice never forms more than 2 inches thick, you can prevent damaging water expansion by floating a piece of styrofoam in the pool. It should be at least a foot square and 2 inches thick.

You can protect smaller ponds in danger of freezing in milder climates by erecting a portable greenhouse over them.

When it comes to protecting fish and plants, move them indoors if the pond is small and likely to freeze solid. Put nonhardy plants in a bucket or other waterproof container under a grow light. Hardy plants don't need light; they'll go dormant. Keep them in buckets of water and limit their exposure to light. Overwinter fish in aquariums if possible (see page 81) or give them away and buy new fish in spring.

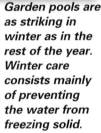

Garden pools are as striking in winter as in the rest of the year. Winter care consists mainly of preventing the water from freezing solid.

In larger ponds, hardy fish and plants can survive the winter if the ice is only a thin sheet. However, if the ice is a constant, solid layer, oxygen won't move into the water and harmful gases will be trapped in it. Hold a pan of boiling water on the surface of the ice until a hole melts through it. Drill thicker ice with an ice auger. Never smash the ice because the vibrations can shock and even kill the fish.

In cold-weather climates, lift water plants that aren't hardy or plants in small water gardens, and store them indoors.

HINT

Fish need more shelter in winter when plant foliage is minimal. A length or two of terra-cotta or PVC pipe at the bottom of the pond will protect them from predators.

TROUBLESHOOTING

PROBLEM: After building the pond, the liner shows.

SOLUTION: First, make sure the pond is full. If that doesn't solve the problem, and if practical, disassemble the edging and re-lay it to make it level with the water surface. Dig soil out from underneath the edge of flexible liner to lower the edging. If necessary, add additional edging material or stone, making sure it overlaps the edging and disguises the exposed liner.

Consider planting evergreens or other sprawling plants alongside the edge to help conceal the liner. They will provide a cosmetic fix as well as protect the liner from UV rays.

PROBLEM: Fish are dying.

SOLUTION: Make sure fish aren't overstocked. There should be just 2 to 3 inches of fish per square foot of surface (see page 81).

If fish have been "gulping" at the surface, they are suffering from lack of oxygen. Install a pump with an air stone or aerator, or add a trickle of cool (75° F) water.

Disease may also be the culprit. Observe the fish, removing them to a bucket of pond water if necessary. Signs of disease include sluggishness, clamped fins, hovering in a corner or at the bottom of the pond, abnormal blotching or markings, and ragged fins or tails. Take the fish to a professional for further diagnosis and treatment.

PROBLEM: Muddy water remains for several hours to a day after a heavy rain.

SOLUTION: Muddy water, in itself, is usually not a problem, especially if the silt settles within a few hours. The problem, however, could be caused by soil erosion or mud splashed into the pond by heavy rain. You should check around the water feature, especially at its edging. Spread any eroding or rain-splashed soil with gravel, organic mulch, or plant a ground cover in the problem area.

PROBLEM: The water level drops and the pond leaks.

SOLUTION: Pool repair kits are readily available. To repair a pond, drain it with a pump or siphon and locate the leak. Remove anything that might have punctured the liner, such as stones or sticks. Back the puncture or tear, if possible, with damp sand or pond underlayment. Then clean and dry the surface areas completely. Using a pond liner adhesive and following repair kit instructions, spread a generously sized patch (at least 2 inches longer and wider than the leak) with adhesive and attach it. Let the patch dry before refilling the pond.

PROBLEM: My submersible pump quit operating after just a few months.

SOLUTION: With proper care, a good-quality water-garden pump should last for several years. For longest life, make sure debris or algae doesn't tax its motor. Clean the prefilter or intake filter at least once a week during the spring and up to three times a week in summer and fall. Make sure the pump isn't sitting directly on the pond bottom, where it will take in more silt. Set it on a brick or flat stone. If algae clogs the pump, clean the pump and make an additional filter by wrapping the pump in a large piece of fiberglass window screen, then place it inside a black plastic basket. Never run the pump without water. It will burn out the motor.

PROBLEM: The water has a foul smell.

SOLUTION: Bad smells from your pond mean that anaerobic bacteria (those that don't use oxygen) have gotten out of hand. A buildup of anaerobic bacteria could be caused by poor aeration, a dead animal in the water, or an excess of uneaten fish food.

Add a waterfall or a pump (or increase pump volume) to increase aeration. Promptly remove dead or decaying plant matter and dead fish. Minimize fish feeding, and don't feed at all during hot weather. Keep the water feature topped off in warm weather so the water doesn't get murky. Finally, reevaluate your ecosystem—adding filtering plants may help. In severe cases, a biological water filter (see page 26) may be the solution.

PROBLEM: The area where I want to build a pond is filled with tree roots.

SOLUTION: If the area is full of roots, you'll need to move the pond location to one outside the tree's dripline—the circular area covered by the spread of the branches—or build an aboveground pool.

If the tree is mature and has only a few roots that are no more than an inch or two in diameter in the area you plan to install the pool, you can cut them with loppers or a saw. If you run into a large root that is more than 2 inches in diameter, you can saw it off, but don't cut more than one or two of these big roots or you'll risk injuring the tree. Never significantly reduce the number of roots for either young or mature trees; you can injure the tree, put it at risk for disease, or kill it.

PROBLEM: Portions of my water plants brown and die.

SOLUTION: Some dieback and loss of leaves is natural. Regularly trim off yellowing or browning plant material to keep the plants healthy and the water clear.

PROBLEM: In autumn, I try to keep up with scooping out fallen leaves, but I can't.

SOLUTION: Fallen leaves need to be removed almost daily so they don't have a chance to decay and pollute the water. If your pool or pond is located under a tree or regularly collects fallen leaves, consider stretching netting over the pond to catch the leaves. Anchor the netting on the side with bricks or stakes driven into the soil. Be sure to remove these netted leaves regularly so they don't shade the water.

If the leaves have sunk to the bottom, they can be removed with your hand or with a soft plastic rake. For larger pools, especially those without many plants or fish, consider investing in a pool sweep, which attaches to a garden hose and uses water pressure to remove debris and silt from the pond bottom. A spa vacuum will also work. Both are available from water-garden suppliers.

PROBLEM: My fish don't seem hungry.

SOLUTION: Particularly in the late spring through early fall, fish usually have enough food—mosquito larvae, plants, and other insects—in their habitat to keep them satisfied. They can easily go without any external feeding during this time.

The problem may be that you're feeding them too much. Fish should always seem ravenous when you feed them. Otherwise, they don't eat all the food and the excess becomes pond waste.

Also, make sure you're feeding the fish the appropriate food. Avoid foods not made specifically for outdoor ornamental pond fish. Feed fish on a regular schedule; the best time is in the afternoon, from midday to an hour before sunset.

PROBLEM: I need to divide my water-garden plants, but they won't budge out of their plastic pots.

SOLUTION: The easiest way to remove a pot-bound water-garden plant is to cut away the plastic pot with a hand shears.

Once out of the pot, severely pot-bound plants can still be difficult to break apart into divisions. Remove soil by spraying them with a strong stream of water so you can see how the roots are configured. Then try to break the rootball apart with a pruning fork. If that doesn't work, insert a second fork back to back with the first into the rootball. Pry the two handles apart. If this doesn't work, slice through the roots with a spade.

PROBLEM: I have a small, bathtub-sized water garden with a fountain. I want to keep fish, but they always die after a couple of weeks.

SOLUTION: It may be that there's too much current in the pond. Especially in container and other very small water gardens, there should be an area with no current so that fish don't become stressed. Reduce the current by turning the flow adjuster. If the fountain's nozzle is supposed to be underwater, make sure it is indeed just under or as much as an inch under the surface.

Fall colors are lovely around a garden pool. Be sure to skim fallen leaves from the pond daily to avoid problems.

FREQUENTLY ASKED QUESTIONS

Q: Won't a water garden be the perfect breeding ground for mosquitoes?

A: A neglected or badly planned water garden can indeed be a haven for mosquitoes. But you can prevent mosquitoes in a couple of ways.

First, make sure the water moves. A strong fountain or splashing waterfall can take care of that.

Second, stock the water feature—even just a tub—with fish, especially goldfish (or mosquito fish in small water gardens). They eat mosquito larvae.

Q: Our city water has chlorine and various minerals in it. Can I use that in my water garden or do I have to find a special source?

A: Chlorine dissipates from the water in just a few days, or you can add a dechlorinator. After filling your water garden, let it sit for five to seven days before adding plants and fish. Minerals in your drinking water are fine.

More of a concern to water gardeners are chloramines, which are added to (or occur naturally in) many local water supplies. Call the water supplier to ask if they are present. If they are, treat your water with a special chloramine remover before adding fish.

Q: I'm considering hiring a professional to help me design my water garden, but how can I tell if the person is qualified?

A: A trained horticulturist, landscape designer, or landscape architect may be of some help. But water gardening as practiced today is a fairly new and highly specialized area—something that is not yet taught in classrooms. First, ask for a portfolio so you can get an idea of how well-designed the water features will be. Then, have the designer supply you with the names and numbers of two or three previous clients that you can contact to make sure their water gardens are still going strong and that the specialist is reliable and professional.

Q: My water lily didn't bloom this year. What did I do wrong?

A: Failure of a water lily to bloom can be caused by several things. Overcrowded roots in the pot can be one reason the lily doesn't bloom. Check to see if roots are pushing out the sides or top of the container or if they're packed in so tightly that they're distorting the container. If so, divide the plant and repot it.

Also, check light levels. Lilies are sunlovers, requiring at least 6 hours of full sun each day. Any less and blooms will be diminished.

Make sure, too, that the lily isn't getting too much competition from other water lilies or deep-water plants or floaters. Keep yellowing or dying foliage trimmed to help the plant devote as much energy as possible into blooming.

Q: What happens if the power goes out? Will my fish die?

A: If the power goes out for just a few hours, even in hot weather, your fish should be fine. However, if the power is out for several days, the fish might become stressed for lack of oxygen. If they show signs of stress—gulping at the water surface—install a battery-powered air pump to aerate the water. If you plan to keep expensive fish, it's especially wise to invest in an air pump or a generator for just such emergencies.

Q: Exactly how do I overwinter fish indoors? Can I just put them in a bucket in the basement?

A: An aquarium is ideal because it allows easy observation, but fish can be kept in just about any clean container that hasn't held detergent or chemicals. Container size depends on the size and number of fish. Figure 1 gallon of water for every inch of fish.

Supply oxygen to the container with an air pump. Keep the water cool, between 45° and 60° F. The water can be allowed to go up to 80° F, but the fish will need to be in containers that hold about 50 percent more water, and you'll need to change the water more frequently and feed the fish more often.

Periodically change 20 percent of the water and keep feeding to a minimum. Fish in the bucket, like fish in the pond, should be ravenous when you feed them. Some fish owners like to set up cool-weather aquariums in their living rooms so that they can enjoy their fish year-round.

GARDEN POOL RESOURCES

Al Zimmer's Ponds & Supplies
6271 Perkiomen Ave.
Birdsboro, PA 19508
800-722-8877
www.azponds.com
Supplies

Avian Aquatics, Inc.
P.O. Box 295
Nassau, DE 19969
800-788-6478
Water features for songbirds

Aqua Art Pond Specialists
11-G PocoWay, Suite 154
American Canyon, CA 94589
800-995-9164 (orderline)
707-642-7663 (Helpline)
www.aquaart.com
Equipment, pond statuary, landscape
accents, and filters

Crystal Palace Perennials, Ltd.
P.O. Box 154
St. John, IN 46373
219-374-9419
www.crystalpalaceperennial.com
Plants. Informative catalog: $3

Gilberg Perennial Farms
2906 Ossenfort Rd.
Glencoe, MO 63038
314-458-2033
Perennial plants and equipment

Green & Hagstrom, Inc.
P.O. Box 658
Fairview, TN 37062
615-799-0708
www.greenandhagstrom.com
Plants and fish, including koi

Lilypons Water Gardens
P.O. Box 10
Buckeystown, MD 21717-0010
800-999-5459
www.lilypons.com
e-mail: info@lilypons.com
Equipment and plants; informative
catalog on items for sale as well as on
the how-to's of water gardening

Lilypons Water Gardens
139 FM 1489
Brookshire, TX 77423-0188

Maryland Aquatic Nurseries, Inc.
3427 North Furnace Rd.
Jarrettsville, MD 21084
410-557-7615
www.marylandaquatic.com
Plants, equipment, fountains for
indoors and out. Catalog features
good pictures and diagrams of filters
and fountains

Paradise Water Gardens
Route 18
Whitman, MA 02382
781-447-4711
www.members.aol.com//ParWtrGnds./
Fish, plants (many unique),
equipment and supplies

Pet Warehouse
P.O. Box 752138
Dayton, OH 45475
800-443-1160
www.petwhse.com; on-line catalog
Some equipment and plants

Scherer Water Gardens
104 Waterside Rd.
Northport, NY 11768
516-261-7432
Fax: 516-261-9325
Fiberglass and polyethylene
preformed pools and EPDM liners.
Other equipment and plants

Signature Ponds, Inc.
418 Liberty Lane
Jasper, GA 30143
706-692-5880
www.mindspring.com//~/sigponds;
on-line catalog.
Lightweight alternative for pond
edge coping stone, boulders and
flat stones

Slocum Water Gardens
1101 Cypress Garden Blvd.
Winter Haven, FL 33884
941-293-7151
Plants, equipment, goldfish and koi
Catalog: $3

Varsity Pond Supplies
2112 Omega Drive
Santa Ana, CA 92705
800-700-1720
e-mail: pspindola@earthlink.net
Tetra Products for ponds and for koi

Van Ness Water Gardens
2460 North Euclid Ave.
Upland, CA 91784-1199
800-205-2425
www.vnwg.com
Catalog: $4
Equipment and plants. In business
since 1932. Catalog offers
information on plant requirements
and their uses and water-gardening
advice

Water Creations
2507 East 21st St.
Des Moines, IA 50317
800-475-2044
Equipment and fish food

Water Garden Gems, Inc.
3136 Bolton Rd.
Marion, TX 78124-6002
800-682-6098
Fax: 210-659-1528
Equipment and some plants. Well-
organized and indexed catalog

Waterford Gardens
74 East Allendale Rd.
Saddle River, NJ 07458
201-327-0721
waterford-gardens.com
Plants, equipment, books, supplies,
fish. Catalog shows true colors of
water lilies and lotus. Catalog: $5

Wildlife Nurseries, Inc.
P.O. Box 2724
Oshkosh, WI 54903-2724
920-231-3780
Hardy, perennial aquatic and wetland
plants, available in quantities of one
to 1,000 stems

William Tricker, Inc.
7125 Tanglewood Dr.
Independence, OH 44131
800-524-3492
One of America's oldest suppliers.
Water lilies, lotus and other water
plants, equipment, books and fish

Water Gardening Magazine
P.O. Box 607
St. John, IN 46373
219-374-9419
www.watergardening.com

INDEX

Page numbers in Italics denote photographs.

THE USDA PLANT HARDINESS ZONE MAP OF NORTH AMERICA

Plants are classified according to the amount of cold weather they can handle. For example, a plant listed as hardy to zone 6 will survive a winter in which the temperature drops to minus 10° F.

Warm weather also influences whether a plant will survive in your region. Although this map does not address heat hardiness, in general, if a range of hardiness zones are listed for a plant, the plant will survive winter in the coldest zone as well as tolerate the heat of the warmest zone.

To use this map, find the approximate location of your community, then match the color band marking that area to the zone key at left.

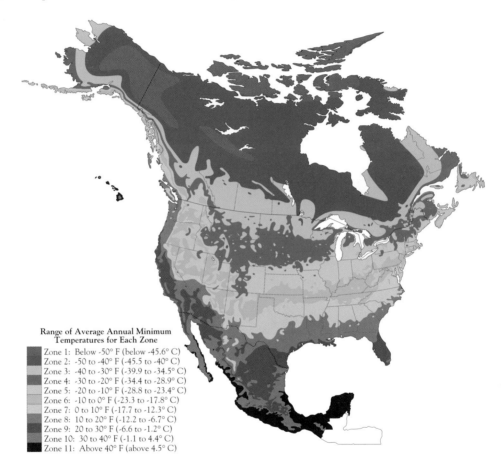

Range of Average Annual Minimum Temperatures for Each Zone

Zone 1: Below -50° F (below -45.6° C)
Zone 2: -50 to -40° F (-45.5 to -40° C)
Zone 3: -40 to -30° F (-39.9 to -34.5° C)
Zone 4: -30 to -20° F (-34.4 to -28.9° C)
Zone 5: -20 to -10° F (-28.8 to -23.4° C)
Zone 6: -10 to 0° F (-23.3 to -17.8° C)
Zone 7: 0 to 10° F (-17.7 to -12.3° C)
Zone 8: 10 to 20° F (-12.2 to -6.7° C)
Zone 9: 20 to 30° F (-6.6 to -1.2° C)
Zone 10: 30 to 40° F (-1.1 to 4.4° C)
Zone 11: Above 40° F (above 4.5° C)

METRIC CONVERSIONS

U.S. Units to Metric Equivalents			Metric Units to U.S. Equivalents		
To Convert From	Multiply By	To Get	To Convert From	Multiply By	To Get
Inches	25.4	Millimeters	Millimeters	0.0394	Inches
Inches	2.54	Centimeters	Centimeters	0.3937	Inches
Feet	30.48	Centimeters	Centimeters	0.0328	Feet
Feet	0.3048	Meters	Meters	3.2808	Feet
Yards	0.9144	Meters	Meters	1.0936	Yards

To convert from degrees Fahrenheit (F) to degrees Celsius (C), first subtract 32, then multiply by ⅝.

To convert from degrees Celsius to degrees Fahrenheit, multiply by ⅝, then add 32.